". . . as it is in Heaven."

True stories about life before life on earth

BY GINNY BROCK

For Julie,

With Love.

Ginny.

First Edition. First printing, 2016

Cover image: Tracey Fulks. Design and layout by Next Generation Designs.

ISBN-13: 978-1534753426

ISBN-10: 1534753427

These are true stories. The incidents surrounding the characters in this book are real and the essence of each story is as it was told to, or experienced by, the author. Names have been changed to protect privacy, and to further protect the participants, the author has, in some cases changed their original locations, ethnicity and gender. Any resemblance to anyone either alive or in spirit, will be obvious to the people who gave me their stories, coincidental to others. It should be noted that all of these stories are similar to countless other stories from all over the world.

Also By Ginny Brock

By Morning's Light

Rainbow Rising

About the Author

Ginny Brock was born in Johannesburg, South Africa, and has travelled extensively throughout her life. She and her American-born husband, Walter, lived and raised a family in many parts of the world including South Africa, The Seychelles Islands, Dubai, Saudi Arabia, Singapore and the United States where she became a naturalized citizen in 1980. She now makes her home at Smith Mountain Lake in Virginia.

If you would like more information about this book, you may contact Ginny Brock at her email address or visit her blog.

Ginny11brock11@gmail.com

www.GINIABROCK.BLOGSPOT.COM

...as it is in Heaven

This book is dedicated to my grandchildren,

and to all the children whose stories are shared here.

*

Special acknowledgement and thanks to the Grown-Ups: young at heart, and not too old to remember and to tell their stories.

Table of Contents

Introduction

When we were young, you and I, we knew things that other people didn't. We could sometimes see things others couldn't and we chatted to people who chatted back; people who no one could hear but us.

This is a compilation of short stories, drawn from many people, but mostly the very young, who still remember where they came from and the friends and animals they've left behind for a lifetime on Earth.

The book begins with a story of a new born, now a middle-aged man, who vividly remembers details of his birth.

He arrived in shock. "Where the bleep am I?" was his first disconnected thought. "Holy—what the heck is this place? Everything's moving and tilting . . . I feel like I'm being lifted! Yikes! They're rotating me! Whoa! What's going on? Hellooo! Can anyone hear me?

This young human spirit, new born and disoriented, is upset. He doesn't remember this place or what it's like down here, and has no immediate memory of how he got here. Although he still remembers the place he's arrived from. The whole transition from an adult spirit to a helpless new born human baby with no idea of where he is, no speech, barely any movement, and sluggishly slow at that, is horrifying to him.

If you believe that we are spiritual beings, who have incarnated on earth to live in human bodies and to learn from being human, then it's not difficult to understand how young children, very recently removed from the place many of us know as "Heaven", still remember that place and the way things are there.

That's what I wanted to know. I wanted to know what they still remember. And I wanted to know who they were with, and what they remember about them.

When I was a young child of four or five years old, I had many fleeting memories of a place I could describe but couldn't quite remember, and I now know that many children have these memories. So, I set about the task of finding out more about them. To do that, I began by talking to my own grandchildren, and then moved on to as many other small humans as I could find before they got too big and busy to want to chat.

You have to move quickly, because unfortunately, as they get older they can lose those memories. I've discovered that as we grow, and our lives become cluttered with mundane things, most of us also lose the inclination and ability to make contact with that world called Heaven. Some of us world-weary travelers still remember bits and pieces of that existence but it's never clear.

And no one real wants to chat about it over cocktails or a cup of tea for fear of talked about. You know, behind the double wide glossy smiles of friends and acquaintances comes a whisper as they look the other way. "She's mad as a hatter, my dear!' sip, sip.

Seriously, you can't really un-friend someone for that I don't think. Heaven knows it's difficult to understand, and that it takes a seismic shift for some to even begin to think about this stuff.

I gave it a lot of thought, and because it doesn't bother me that some think I'm off my rocker or, not playing with a full deck, I launched my own expedition into a world I'd wanted to explore for a long time: The fascinating world of Pre-existence.

I planned the route, took a few wrong turns, located my resources and finally, pulling everything together, and with all systems on Go, I steamed into the project.

The journey began on the back roads of early childhood memories, my own combined with my fellow travelers some of whom were the Newest Arrivals here on earth, but I concentrated on children who were 3-5 years of age. I purposefully chose this age group because they know how to speak. It's the time when they are just beginning to find their way around the language, can express themselves reasonably well, and mostly, love to talk. It is also that purest of times before their minds have become cluttered with a lot of outside information. It's the time when their friendships are limited, opinions don't matter, and the ABC's and the 1,2,3's of life haven't yet begun to complicate things.

I chose this group because they haven't yet learned to fabricate stories. What I got from the three and under set is the unadorned truth. At four, I had to make room for some imagination and sort through the purple dinosaurs and Disney—but four year olds don't lie either. The same goes for five year olds; although a little more discernment had to be used to accommodate some of the mythology provided by wise and all-knowing contemporaries.

Other accounts were given to me by parents, close relatives, teachers and pediatric nurses. All of them, people I trusted implicitly because I could see no reason for them to make up any of this.

My research was more rewarding than I could have imagined. It turned up pages and pages of extraordinary, heart-warming, jaw dropping, wide-eyed, funny and also poignant accounts and memories.

Children *get* this stuff, and this book is the end result of over two years of work collecting their stories. There are even a number of memories from some adults who remember imaginary friends of their own. And to this bonanza of information, I have mixed in some of my own experiences with pre-existence, and observations drawn from my own beliefs and intuition.

I am grateful to all who participated in my research. I feel privileged and humbled by their trust in me to present their stories in the very best way I can. And to my Soul self, my Spirit Guides and Angels who set the sign posts that pointed the way, my deepest gratitude.

Have fun with it. Learn from it, be amazed by it, listen with all your senses, and never again dismiss stories like these as 'imagination'! We are the Explorers you and I. And I invite you to join me on this journey of exploration through this world that belongs to the very young, to the new arrivals on our planet; and to those who still remember our pre-existence . . . as it is in Heaven.

…as it is in Heaven

GB

Chapter 1: The Newcomers

Whoa! What's Happening!"

Where am I? Holy . . . What is this place? Everything's moving and tilting. I feel as though I'm being lifted by something or someone and . . . yikes! They're rotating me! Whoa! Help! Somebody help me! What's going on? Helloo? Can anyone hear me? I try to turn and look around but the movement is slow and heavy. My head's so heavy . . . it feels like I'm moving through molasses. Jeese! It feels as though all the blood has rushed to my head. I'm upside down! And someone's pulling on me. What's happening! I can hear something buzzing . . . I'm getting outta here!

I try, but I can't move. There's something blocking my way but I can't figure out what it is. It's kind of tough but soft and I'm feeling myself pushed against it head first! What're they doing?

Then I hear, "That's better, now we've got him–he's turning. He's face down now."

What're they talking about? They've got me! Face down! I'm trapped. Heeelp! I attempt a quick dive looking for an exit but except for a fluttering on my side, I don't move. It feels like I'm a dragon fly stuck in glue or something–I'm scared! Why can't I move . . . Now something's pushing me on both my sides and, *yikes!* They're pinning my arms down! They've stuffed me inside a rubber tube or something. I don't understand. I'm getting desperate. It's like being in the middle of one of those nightmares I used to get!

Now I'm being pulled upwards by unseen forces and suddenly I'm cold all over. Then just as I'm about to lose it, something loud slams into me leaving a stinging sensation behind–and there's a sound I know I've heard before. The sound goes on–and then it comes to me; it's a human baby crying! There's a baby around here! Someone has hurt a baby! I can feel heat and that stinging sensation rising from somewhere behind me, lower down my being.

Oh, no! I'm starting to remember. It strikes me with such force that I almost choke. Truth is stranger than fiction, my friends. I've made the transition into a human being and it was my baby bottom that just got slammed! Now they're shoving something down my throat that feels as though it's pulling me inside out with this gurgling, sucking noise!

"There!" I hear a soft voice crooning, and a large face comes close to mine. "Now you're okay, little man! We got that nasty ol' stuff you choked on. There, there, you're okay now."

That's what she thinks! I am NOT okay. This is all a mistake! How did I get into this fix? As I lie there, it seems as though this fog I'm swimming in begins to lift and slowly, a stream of memories creeps in. Snippets of conversations flood my being. Forgotten faces drift in and out of the mist and I'm remembering long hours spent in decision making with people I once knew; friends and Guides who helped me make the decision to come to earth. The realization hits me like a wave of ice cold water. What was I thinking? There must be some mistake . . . I can't move . . . my normal thought passages don't work, I used to be able to think my way out of things but now they're blocked! My being no longer responds to thoughts that used to allow me to come and go as I please–to move anyway I wanted to, to be somewhere else just by thinking it . . . what bliss! Now all of that is gone. Just when I need it most. I'm having a panic attack.

Then the baby cries again. I can hear the sound of loud human voices and hurried footsteps. I try to tell them to slow down, for Pete's sake. They're scaring me. I forgot they have such loud voices. Hey! You don't have to shout .

. . Can't you see, I'm right here? Just don't slap me again! And keep that plumbing tool away from me!

Cold hands turn my baby body over onto its front. I feel it's trying to open its eyes. What's that sticky stuff all around them? Everything looks fuzzy; it's like rising to the surface through a pool of murky water. Everything's blurred. This is the end! I used to be able to see clearly–way beyond and behind things. Now there's a big human body in my line of vision blocking my view of what's behind it. I used to be able to see through things like this. Looks like that's a thing of the past too.

I wait, tell myself to take a deep breath. Calm down. I've got to think! Then I call out to someone I used to know; someone who'll get me out of this mess. But no one answers, and I remember; my thoughts are blocked. These earthlings have blocked my thoughts and the baby's started to cry again.

"Don't worry, little fellow," I try my hardest to project my thoughts. "Someone will come and rescue us . . . you'll see." This is chaotic!

The panic's rising. No one can hear me. Then all of a sudden, just as I'm about to lose it I feel a warm flutter on my cheek and for a moment a deep calm has entered my space. It feels like I used to feel before I had this really bad idea of being born on earth for another round of humanity. "Is that you?" I think of someone I loved a lot before I got to this place. There's no answer, nothing but the honey smooth warmth of calm that enfolds me at this moment. It's seeped through the veil that now separates me from where I used to be. They said that would happen . . .

The people seemed to have moved away from me. I can hear metallic-like sounds mingling with their loud voices. There's also this drumming sensation—a rhythmic beating and I think it's coming from inside me. For a moment I'm scared again. 'Scared' is another feeling I forgot about. I don't like this scared feeling. I try to think of that peaceful honey calm. Perhaps if I can just calm down all of this will go away.

Go with the flow. That was a good thought it seems because the baby has stopped crying, and as I lie there taking in this bizarre scene, things begin to clear up. The thumping in my chest stops thumping so fast and I can even see more clearly.

A shadow falls over me. Darn! There they go again— someone's turning my body. Why do they keep doing that! What do they think they're doing? They're twisting and poking me. I don't like it. Hey! Leave me alone. Keep your hands off me!

My baby whimpers and then he's quiet. They must have turned us right side up because the images I'm starting to see floating before me aren't upside-down anymore. Everything's upright now including a large figure right in front of me who's wearing something bright on its head that makes me want to close my eyes. It's a light! That's it! I remember lights. Have I been here before? Now he's aimed that light into my eyes. He's looking inside me! Me. I thought me! Whoa! I'm beginning to identify with the human being whose body I'm in. The baby. Me! I'm the baby! This is my new body! I'm in my earth baby's body!

My new vision is picking up something else going on, off to the side. It's an individual covered in white. Just her hands and face are showing above a starched collar and long sleeves. There's something on her head. It's not a light . . . It's like wings, sharp pointy wings that come from the top of her head. It's some sort of special hat. She must be someone special but why is she wrapped in all that hard and pointy white stuff? She's staring at me through big glasses–dark horn-rimmed glasses!

I try turning my head towards her and I hear the sounds of metal clanking on metal. I try my eyes again and see that they move quite well. That's a relief! That thing they swiped over my face must have cleaned up the sticky stuff in my eyes because I'm looking at something that looks like a silver tray with shiny instruments clanking around on it. 'Clanking' is a sound! A sound! And then I become aware of other sounds. There are loud sounds all around me. I hear a snapping sound that's comes from a silver thing that snaps open and shut in her hand. It's scissors—*yikes!* How do I know that? She's pointing them at me! I try to bolt but nothing happens. Then there's a loud, dull 'click'. Whoa! I've been unplugged! Disconnected. I'm loose! And just as I'm about to put this new freedom to good use and flee from this nightmare, I feel those white arms lift me up with a crackling sound and carry me through the air before placing me on something soft and warm. I can hear muffled voices saying words I can't make out. I want to talk to them but just as I'm about to say something I think they need to hear, I remember that my earth baby doesn't know the words yet.

This is not good at all. I hope this baby guy's a fast learner or this is going to be a very long life. I try to tell them to look at me. I can beam thoughts to them if they will. But they can't hear me, and that's because you have to use your human voice here. It's all coming back. They apparently have very little, if any, knowledge of things like thought transference or telepathy. No one can 'hear' you.

So I go on a search for my human voice. I find it. It's a queer little sound that comes from somewhere below my head. I try to pull it upwards, and as I do, my baby mouth opens and out comes this yell! It's different from the crying sound I heard before. I like it, so I try it again. It comes out much louder this time and the people turn to look at me. That's more like it! One of them is leaning close to my face again making strange noises.

I can see something else, too. It's smooth and it feels warm on the side of my face. It's the color of raw silk and I like the soft smell. I turn my face and feel it warm and giving against my skin. It feels very safe–and I can hear a soft voice comforting me. It's a voice I recognize. It's almost, almost . . . I can't see her face, but somehow I'm very sure it's her. It's the voice I've been hearing for some time. It's her! My earth mother!

I want to talk to her, but when I try, the baby cries again! Of course it does! It can't speak. I try again and it cries louder. So loud it scares me. I want my mother!

That's a new feeling. Then I hear someone, making soft mouth noises. I like that . . . she's speaking. She's a large soft being with long hair, dark and shiny, that falls over one of her shoulders. Her gentle touches replace the roughness I sensed earlier and I can feel her gather my baby in. It feels nice to be held so close. I feel protected, warm and I'm filled with feelings of love. I had forgotten these feelings of human love. They make my baby squirm and snuggle into this warm and sweet-smelling being that must be my mother. Then I hear her speak. She says "Hi, little Baby Trevor. Welcome to the world."

"Hmmm. 'Trevor'. I like that.

~

As Trevor grew up, he never forgot that memory of his birth. When he thought about it as a child, or as a young adult, he thought it must have been a dream. What else could it be? But as he got older he began to realize that it wasn't a dream but something that was real. It was the memory of a real-life experience.

How could he possibly have 'dreamed' up the scenario of an old-fashioned delivery room and unfamiliar hospital uniforms? And the words and language he couldn't understand. Why was he 'dreaming' upside-down? When it finally dawned on him, he realized that if you're being born head first, being held upside down, everything around you would almost certainly be upside down. This was certainly no dream, but a memory. It could only be a memory of a real-life experience.

~

To clarify the language of spirituality, a 'young' spirit is not young in years as we understand time. The term is used for spirits who have had little or no experience with an incarnation on earth, so they have scant memories of what it's like to live in our dimension. They make the decision to come to earth for a variety of reasons. One may be that this is a challenging environment for even the strongest among us. It may be the original 'school of hard knocks. ' And as such, it is where we can earn a lot of kudos for the next world.

In contrast, an 'Old' spirit is one who has been here many times before, one who takes it all in stride, settling in like an old hand, probably thinking, "I've got this!" There are no surprises for an old spirit because he's done it all before and he or she remembers what it was like and what to expect.

Chapter: 2 Rosa

"I would dream of flying . . ."

All wrapped up and swaddled under the bright lights of an earthly delivery room, I lay there thinking, and the first thought that came to mind was that I knew this place. My memory of the last time I was here was sharp, and I also knew I didn't want to be here. But just like before, there was no turning back now.

It felt barren and cold and I was unhappy, just like before. I hadn't felt unhappy since the last time I was here. There was no unhappiness in the place I had just left. But old memories of earth were coming back, rolling through the strangeness of it all, and I knew what to expect and I felt like crying.

The vibrations were so heavy here. It felt like a brooding thunderstorm descending. I didn't want this human form–so limited in every way. My chest got heavy with the weight of despair, I felt as though I was drowning and I began to whimper.

This new body was a real nuisance. When all I wanted to do was to rise up out of this swampy place and all it could do was just lie there like a block of soft, wet clay. I longed for what I'd left behind. I used to be a whisper of a being; a vastly intelligent gossamer being–a strand of light– lighter than air. All of my thoughts and intentions used to have invisible wings that became my mode of transportation and flying games and journeys were the most fun.

It wasn't hard to guess that my flying days were on hold for the time being. It would take me a long time to learn to even walk efficiently, I thought with a shudder remembering the shocking landings of before. I would have to drag this poor human form around everywhere I went. There would be scrapes and bruises and hurt feelings, and years and years of learning to figure it all out.

But I would dream of flying, and in those dreams I soar and remember how it really is.

~

It wasn't an experience that the baby girl relished, but she knew there were things left undone from the last time she was on earth. Memories of her last trip through the veil began to crowd her thoughts, making her want to leave, to forget she'd ever decided to come back.

~

All I wanted was to be back in that place of soft light where it was easy to be happy, and laughter, joy and unconditional love were woven indelibly into the fabric of being. Most of all I wanted to be with those I'd had left behind. I missed them with a yearning that seemed unbearable. They would miss me too, I knew that. So what the heck made me do this! They would be sad for me, watching me struggle and they would understand what I was feeling, but all they could do would be to reassure me and hope I heard them through the thin veil that separated us. They would do what they could but they also knew, as I did, that I'd chosen this lifetime for a reason and they would not interfere.

The Elders called it, The Evolvement of my Spirit, which sounded good at the time, but now I'm wondering why the heck my Spirit needed evolving anyway. This was a fine state of affairs. But what was there to do but to get on with this life?! So it was going to be up to me. And as small and pathetic as I felt, I was just going to have to get on with things and get busy living being human.

The only spark of light in all this was that even though my friends wouldn't interfere with my choices, they'd be close by. All I had to do would be to call out when things got bad and they would be there to help. But it wouldn't be the same.

I especially longed for the wise and gentle beings who had counseled me while I was deciding whether to come into this new earth life or not. Just wait until I see them again. I'd have to let them know we'd made a terrible choice! I longed for their reassurance and their wisdom and their strength because I felt neither wise nor strong in this cold and inhospitable dimension.

And another thing! The smells here were atrocious. They were sharp smells that made my nose run and stung my eyes. The lights were too bright . . . I felt pain in my right arm where the pressure of physical birth had cramped it. And I was sounding like a moaning Minnie! But who could blame me?

There was no doubt I was on Earth. I'd definitely made it through the veil or I wouldn't be experiencing all these physical sensations and acting like a miserable changeling. Something else I noticed was that with every second that passed I felt myself experiencing more and more of the human being I was becoming, brought here for yet another lifetime in this difficult earth school. I lay there motionless for a while wallowing in misery. And then I had a thought.

I had an ace up my sleeve! Ah, Ha! Yes! I knew for a fact that if things got ridiculously bad I could leave this place and be home in a snap. It was a simple matter of taking one of those exit points the counselors had talked about before I left. *"Use them if things get too hard to bear,"* I remembered them saying. I remember that well, and the temptation to grab an exit point was almost too much to resist. All I had to do was to stop breathing and I'd be home.

At the same time, I had a nagging feeling, that there was a compelling reason I had made the decision to reincarnate. In fact, I knew that. There was something I was supposed to do. The only trouble was I couldn't remember what that was or anything about it. My memory was getting worse by the minute. They had told me this would happen. You weren't born into humanity knowing what to expect or what you were supposed to do. The earth life had a way of unfolding and revealing what you needed to know when the time was right. It probably wouldn't be very long, before everything I now remembered about the place I came from, would be forgotten. Even my friends . . . I was getting scared. Very scared, and I could feel my human body reacting.

~

The baby girl squeezed her eyes tight, opened her mouth and started to sob. Then almost as quickly, she stopped. Someone was singing. She knew that sound and as she listened, her sobs subsided and she looked around the place she was in. A large human form was holding her and making that pleasing singing sound. Something in the sound of the song calmed her and made her feel secure.

~

I knew that sound, didn't I? It was a sound so sweet, so soft . . . As soon as I felt that forgotten feeling of human pleasure, I almost jumped for joy—making the baby jerk and flail its arms—and then, out of nowhere, I knew, don't ask me how, that this time around I was going to be doing something fun. My life's purpose, this time around, would be one of bringing joy to people. I tried everything I could to hold on to that thought, groping around in my new mind for strands of the gossamer-like memory, clinging to it, even as it slipped in and out of focus, knowing somehow that it would be a long time before I had that thought again.

The people around me were smiling and clapping. It seemed as though the applause was for me . . . I wanted to laugh and clap with them, but I wasn't nearly that accomplished.

I liked the sound of clapping! This whole thing was getting better.

But even as I thought about it, it was fading. And even as the earthly sound continued, the memory of what it conveyed vanished. I tried as hard as I could to bring it back but I couldn't find it. All knowledge of my origin and my current life's purpose was slipping rapidly behind the veil.

~

"Welcome to my world," said the now grown-up Rosa as she laughed out loud. A belly laugh with spectacular projection, you wouldn't expect from someone as small as she was. She paused for a minute, thinking. Then she said, "When I look back on my life now, I wonder at how everything just fell into place–almost as though it was all planned out in advance.

"From the time I was quite young, I was drawn to music and dance and now, when I look back, my whole life revolves around it. I love to sing," she said wistfully, "My mother forced me into the choir at church with flattering remarks like, 'But, Rosa you have such a lovely voice!' As she dragged the hairbrush through my tangled mass of hair I wouldn't let anyone cut. Then there were piano lessons and when I started high school, the first thing I did was to join the glee club and after that, I never looked back."

The Universe works in strange ways. Through her next door neighbor, Rosa was introduced to the home health nurse who told a nursing home director about her, and, now in her middle years, Rosa works with nursing homes, counseling and singing to them; bringing them a few hours of happiness. "And that, has brought me untold happiness," She remarked.

"Ever the actress, there are times I dress up like The Cat in the Hat, or a Box Car Willy outfit or a Charlie Chaplin get up and act out for them. Nobody boos or charges for the exits, they just hug me and give me valentines on February 14th every year! And at the end of the performances they clap and clap and clap."

~

As she lives out her life's purpose, Rosa has never forgotten that memory of her birth or lost that spiritual awareness she felt so strongly on the day she was born. Then, as now, she was and is, often aware of her consciousness being drawn to higher levels as the thinly veiled memories seep in.

"It's useful," she says pensively. "I work with that knowledge, and use it in my counseling. I also find that my intuition has remained sharp all my life and that too is invaluable. It works wonders in my work as an Integrative Intuitive Counselor, where I can incorporate spiritual teachings and writing. And that memory of my birth is still a part of everything I do. It's comforting to me, and sometimes it lets me speak of the place we'll all go back to some day—and that's comforting for others."

~

I guess it's all a matter of that degree of awareness that decides what we remember and what we don't, and whether or not an individual retains any of it—throughout the person's life, or not. So, if you've ever wondered where we come from, and how we got here and even why we came, ask a child.

Chapter 3: Ask a Child

"Will you introduce me to your friend? The one

only you can see."

We're taught by all the major religions of the world, East and West, that we have an eternal soul or spirit, or Higher Self. They teach about an afterlife when we leave this earth. It's strange to me that not many of them teach about a life before life. Or pre-existence.

Children who remember other lives, signal to me and to countless others who have held these conversations with them, and yes, with babies yet to be born, that we were alive long before we were born on earth. We are so much more than a group of cells that came together all of a sudden in the warm depths of somebody's womb and began to turn and churn and grow into a human being. And as if that isn't miraculous enough, it is a fact that we are so much more than that.

You may be lucky enough to know a child who has an 'imaginary' or invisible friend. If you do, I hope you won't miss the opportunity to get involved and do some sleuthing. Tread carefully, you're on sacred ground here, and the tenor of the conversation you're having with such a child, is as flighty as a flame. Burning brightly one minute snuffed the next.

Keep it simple, is my mantra; asking questions clearly and directly, such as, 'What's your friend's name?' Or 'Will you introduce me to your friend?' Children are naturally direct, and will pick up any overt attempt you might make to interrogate. So tread lightly around the nuances and veiled questions. They'll bust you if you don't.

If you strike gold, and manage to engage the child, you will be lead down one of the most fascinating pathways of childhood there is, where you may find yourself in something of a role reversal, with the youngster leading the way. Let her. You have no idea where this will lead but, if you listen carefully, follow hopefully and with confidence, you will be shown things you simply cannot write off as 'imaginary'.

There even are instances, if you're very lucky, when you don't have to do anything but sit and listen as the child reveals this magical other world to you, with no encouragement necessary.

In the next story, one uncle stumbled into one of these encounters, initiated by the child, without having to do any sleuthing at all. In fact, nothing was further from his mind until Sally re-introduced him to an old friend of his, by way of a Hippo.

Chapter 4: Sally

A Guest at Sally's Tea Party

That uncle was my friend Jon, who told me about an intriguing conversation he once had with his niece many years ago. It happened while he was visiting his sister and her four year old daughter in a neighboring state, and during his stay, he told me, "I was invited to Sally's tea party, along with two of her dolls and a stuffed hippo that had once belonged to me. When I asked my sister where that had come from, she said that she'd rescued several of our old toys from the rag bin, sentimentally packing them away for the next generation.

At tea time that day, while stuffing my adult bulk into an impossibly tiny chair, Sally introduced me to herself, Lady Sally, and then introduced me to our assortment of toy companions, including my hippo who she had named Hip Hop. It was a rather off-beat name for a hippo, I thought. But remembering my tea party manners, I made no comment.

"Say hello to Lord Jon," Sally reminded them, and turned her attention on me. "My mom told me that Hip Hop was your hippo when you were little," she said matter-of-factly as she lifted a tiny teacup off the tray and filled it with invisible tea.

I remarked that that was so, and when I did, my niece put her tea cup down very carefully and said, "But mommy didn't know, and I didn't tell her, that it really belonged to Jamie."

"What!" I stammered.

"That's right," the little girl said patiently. "Jamie told me he left it at your house one night and you never gave it back to him."

Well! You could have knocked me over with a pink plastic teacup. You see, Jamie, my childhood friend, was killed in the Vietnam War years before that and I had completely forgotten the hippo incident, years and years ago. She handed me a teacup and as I sat there gathering my wits, I asked her, "How do you know about Jamie?"

"I just know him," she replied. "Here baby doll, take a sip and don't spill it on your dress." Sally held a pink teacup to the doll's mouth.

24

"Do you see him often? I mean . . ." I was stuck for words

"Sometimes, but not much,' she said with a patient sigh. "He told me you were coming to tea, and then he told me about Hip Hop."

This was beginning to feel like the Mad Hatter's tea party. Any minute now, I'd could shrink to the size of an acorn and disappear down a rabbit hole. Note to self, 'Stay away from the mushrooms.'

I picked up my tea cup and gulped a mouthful of air. "Does your mom know that the hipp– excuse me, Hip Hop, once belonged to Jamie?"

"No, silly!" she laughed. "Jamie says only you an' me know."

"I see," was my uninspired reply, but it was the best my addled brain could come up with.

"Here, Uncle Jon," Sally handed me an empty saucer. "Have a piece of cake. Are you coming to see my new school tomorrow? Eat your Angel cake."

"Thank you, your ladyship," I murmured, relieved that the conversation was over. I took a deep breath and swallowed a lump of invisible Angel Food cake.

~

That evening, after a late dinner on the patio, as I helped my sister clear off the table I turned to her and, feeling a little disloyal to my niece, dropped an innocent sounding remark into the sound of water running in the sink, "During our afternoon tea party, Sally introduced me to Hip Hop,"

She laughed. "How do you like the name? The image of Hip Hop the hippo makes me laugh."

"Did you ever know anything about the line of possession surrounding that hippo?" I asked

"What do you mean?" She grabbed a bottle of Windex from the cabinet and a rag from the rag bin. "I know he belonged to you."

"I'm talking about my misspent youth," I said. "Jamie left it at our house after a sleepover and I'm sorry to say, I kept it–knowingly. I kept his hippo. I even helped him look for it–knowing full well it was hidden under the bed."

She paused whatever she was doing and standing there with the cloth in mid-air she said, "You stole Jamie's hippo?"

"Yup."

She put her hands on her hips and laughed. "You had me fooled. I always thought it was yours, now you're telling me my little brother is a master thief?"

"Was. I didn't think he liked the hippo much," I said lamely.

"What made you think of Jamie after all these years— other than you were re-introduced to the hippo?"

"Brace yourself, Sis. Sally told me she knew that Hip Hop belonged to Jamie before I took him." I winced. "*Stole* him, if you prefer. That's what made me think you had said something to her."

"No, I didn't. And what on earth are you talking about? How in the world did she know about Jamie? I've never spoken about him to her. Have you?" She turned back to the sink. "No, of course not . . . Why would you."

"Of course not," I parroted. "Jamie died six or seven years before Sally was born.'

"Where on earth could she have picked up such a thing? Strange isn't the word for it! Well, whatever, let's not encourage her." My sister shook her head and stared at me. "I don't know what to say!"

With that, she turned and busied herself scrubbing at the stove, so I let the subject drop.

~

Is it possible that Sally and Jamie knew each other before Sally was born? It happens more often than we know that people they've known before they came to earth will show up in spirit form to talk to a child. Are these the 'imaginary friends' we hear children talking to?

As one parent I know has said, "It's so odd, I think of my mother every day. I talk to her all the time, and yet, in all the years since she's been gone, I've never seen her! And here's Chloe who's four, telling me she's visiting with grandma!"

When a child is still very new to the world, everything merges together. Not only the new world they're living in but also the world they came from. They almost never differentiate. They live in a fertile environment for exploration and even if someone tries to shut them down when they wander into those fascinating places we can't remember, they remain composed. They know what they know. They'll even tolerate your attitude about not wanting to meet "Joey", because you couldn't see him. They're okay with that usually. But would you set a place at the, table for him, please Mama? If that doesn't work, that's okay too. The child may be disappointed but, now that he's been sent to his room for making up stories, he'll just take Joey with him and make room in his bed for him.

I believe that spirits find it much easier to come through to a child than they do an adult. And I think that's because children are far more receptive than we are. There's no 'push back' or resistance from them. There's no "I must be going crazy! I swear I heard my dad speaking! Oh well, someone call the men in white coats."

A child will see a long-dead grandparent and accept it without question. It makes sense to think that she may have known them on the Other Side, so their visits seem quite natural to her and if these visits happen often enough, the child may even begin to talk about them. As a parent, or grandparent or nosy friend who's writing a book, this is when you should get your Sherlock Holmes tweed cap on, grab the eye glass and listen carefully.

Children are some of our greatest resources for anyone who wants to know about these things. I don't remember my birth but, as a child, I remember thinking about the place I had come from. It began one morning when I four, playing in my nursery. Except for vague household noises, it was quiet in my own small world, when without warning, a thought hit me from out of nowhere. It gave me the biggest jolt of my young life. It was like a bolt of lightning that seemed to leap at me from somewhere far beyond my world. It was, *"What am I doing here?"*

It scared me. What *was* I doing here? And then, Who am I? I froze–terrified. Panic stricken, I ran through the house yelling for my nanny. Searching for something or someone who was solid and familiar, I tried desperately to get a foothold in whatever this place I'd landed in was . . . "Who *am* I Lizzie?" I cried. "What am I doing here?"

Lizzie, a solid mass of light brown, gentle Zulu who smelled of Sunlight soap, picked me up and cradled me in strong arms, telling me that she wasn't sure but she would find out. "I'll ask the *Sangoma*," she said, and because I knew that the wise *Sangomas*, the medicine people, knew everything, I felt sure Lizzie would find the answer.

And she did. "The *Sangoma*, she say, little baby girl spirit suddenly wake up inside you and say, *'What you do here!'* in

30

big voice, and small spirit inside you is *very* afraid to be here on the earth." Lizzie explained. "She a long way from home in the sky, so she scared."

That made sense.

New places still fill me with uncertainty. I've lived in many places and nothing has ever come close to the warm feeling I got from the place I used to live in. It wasn't a place of this earth. I sensed it and felt it, but was never sure where it was, or why I sometimes longed to be back there, back in the soft light, the place where I knew the air could sing in silvery tones, and where the colors of everything I remembered were vibrant and alive

As I grew, I mostly forgot about those odd feelings and thoughts. Just like a little friend I had who once had three invisible friends. When I asked her about them on the day we both started the 3rd grade, she thought about it for a moment and then, with a flip of her hand, she dismissed the question saying, "Oh them . . . they've gone."

As we grow, invisible friends get left behind. Sometimes, we stash them away at somebody else's request.

A mother might say, "It's just your imagination!"Or, a sophisticated seven year old friend might opine, "You're such a baby, if you believe all that!" So we put the thoughts away, and eventually we agree with the sages around us. But if we're lucky we hang on to the shreds and pick them up again later in a much diluted form that we call the Sixth Sense or Intuition. And if we're intuitive enough, we allow that sixth sense to work, especially when we're around our own young children.

Chapter 5: Sidebar

"Talk to me, Pussy Cat . . .

Children and animals have a lot in common, and I mean that in the very best way.

Often, a child and his pet are so close that neither knows where one ends and the other starts. Or who's got the tail and who walks upright. There's a melding of spirits there that makes them feel as though they are one being. It's that Spirit Communication stuff. The fact that they're obviously from two different species, means nothing to either of them. Physicality is no barrier to two like-minded souls who share a communication that we can't fathom.

While we've been talking about children being in touch with Spirits, or invisible friends—you may have noticed that animals do the same thing.

I believe that the clear, uncluttered minds of children and animals allow inter-dimensional sight to exist very easily alongside physical vision. As the Sixth Sense is very much alive and working in some young children, intuition is sharp and focused in animals. It's the same thing. Both children and animals operate on wavelengths that we, as adults, may have put on the back burner.

Animals are uncomplicated. They know what they can see, they trust their senses of smell and hearing and they also know that their friends don't die–animal or human. Who ever thought of such a thing? They know that grandpa, who used to bring treats when he came, still comes to visit and sits in the same old chair he always sat in before he left. They can see him. And there's no one to tell them they're wrong or making things up and pretending. They might get told to stop barking at that chair in the corner, but they don't really take that seriously.

Everyone has heard the story of the dog that waits at the train station for his master to come home, as he always has, only now, his master has passed on and won't be coming home. We think. Or the cat that lies curled up on her deceased owner's favorite sweater leaving it only to eat and take care of her bathroom needs. Could it be that her owner's energy still lingers around that old sweater? And the dog that howls upon its person's passing. There are so many similar stories.

In the rock-solid physical world, this is called 'loyalty' and 'grieving' rather than intuition, but who's to say that dog's master doesn't get off the train every evening to walk home with his dog?

And explain to me why once, when an old friend of mine came to visit, bringing along a friend of hers who had just lost a son, my dog had a very odd reaction.

We were all introduced to each other, including Ranger, my lab, who insisted on being counted, who pushed his way into the group, acknowledging our guest, and raising his head for a pat. Then he waddled off to his mat plopping down with a grunt, put his head between his paws and closed his eyes. Normal Ranger behavior.

Then we sat down in the living room and exchanged the usual pleasantries, "Ah, You're from North Carolina. What brings you here?" that sort of thing. Until the subject of her loss was brought up. It was apparent that her grief was still raw and that she missed the boy very much. So, I made her a cup of tea. A cup of tea is the cure-all for everything that has been passed down on the female side of my family for generations. "Had a bad day? Have a cuppa tea, dear." Or after a fall, "I think my leg's broken!" and the predictable reply was, "Oh dear. I'll make a pot of tea. Don't worry, dear, everything's alright."

As she sipped her tea and talked about her son, Ranger got up from his mat and very quietly, walked over to where our guest was sitting and put his head on her lap. She stroked his head and kept talking. She must have liked dogs, and that was a good thing because he didn't move away from her all afternoon; alternating between laying his head on her lap and flopping across her feet on the floor.

He ignored me for the most part, and ignored my old friend–someone whose visits he always enjoyed. He seemed to gravitate, as if pulled by some ancient string of intuition to our grieving companion's side.

He definitely he picked up on her sadness. Could he hear it in her voice? Or see it in her eyes? Was he reading her body language? It was possibly all of the above. But have you thought that her son's spirit might have been with us that afternoon? Is it possible that he communicated to Ranger that his mother could use a little puppy love right now? To Ranger, the conversation would have seemed very natural.

~

The thing that makes it easier for animals to hold onto their natural instincts is that nobody messes with their intuition. We usually don't pay much attention to it. And they, for the most part, don't care. No one tells them they're crazy so they go on believing in themselves and following their strong intuitive urgings, and, I believe, they travel effortlessly from one dimension to another.

Dogs just take things as they come and don't worry much about anything. Cats on the other hand, are right on top of these things, switched on and tuned in all the time, even when you think they're sleeping. They are clairvoyant, clairaudient and clairsentient! They get it all. Not only do they see invisible beings, and hear things that we don't, if you've ever owned one, you'll know that they can also read your thoughts.

For instance: I woke up one morning and the first thing that popped into my mind was that Miss Kitty had to go to the vet that day for shots. The appointment was made a week ago, out of earshot of the cat. (You have to do that) So, I lay there with my eyes closed, not moving a muscle, making silent plans around the 3:00 p.m. visit.

This may sound simple, but the first thing I had to remember, was *don't think too loudly! She'll pick up*. And do not make eye contact.

The next thing I had to remember was to get her cat carrier out of the closet while she wasn't looking. *Very quietly*.

So, sticking to my resolve not to think loudly, or even softly, I fed her mindlessly and made the mistake of giving her beef pate instead of tuna flakes. She was not amused. So, I apologized like some sort of bullied waitress, and changed the menu.

She was happy and purring like a miniature motor car. Then she finished it up and flopped in a sunny spot on the carpet to resume her daytime nap.

Still operating mindlessly I opened the hall closet while she was nose down in the carpet, to extract the cat carrier. I picked up the box and tiptoed into the hallway.

She didn't see me. She's oblivious to the plot at hand, I thought. Slowly, and oh so quietly, I placed the carrier on the hall table and hummed a little tune (that had nothing to do with vets or cat carriers) and wandered in to see if she was still asleep.

She had one eye open and it oozed evil intent.

"What is it, Kitty?" I asked innocently.

She growled, fixed me with a malignant stare and dove out of sight.

WHAT! But it was too late. I knew that Miss Kitty would stay out of sight all morning, and only a lot of loud shaking of the cookie box would bring her out of hiding. And not a word has been uttered about any vet appointment.

~

On the night of the day my husband passed away, both Ranger and Miss Kitty abandoned their regular sleeping places and came into my bedroom. Ranger flopped down beside the bed and Miss Kitty jumped up and lay beside me, purring all night long. She had never done that before.

Animals, like children, KNOW things. So, with that in mind, I set off into unchartered waters, to find a few children who would talk to me, and invite me into that wonderful world that is theirs. The one we grownups seldom get to explore.

Chapter 6: Rebecca

". . . and before you were born, Boo? Where were you then?" I
asked.

"A Place . . ." She said.

I waited. "Can you tell me about it?'

She nodded.

It was my first intentional probe into a time and place I can no
longer remember, and for the occasion I chose my granddaughter
Rebecca. She was four years old at the time, right in the
middle of that good age, that window, between three and
five, when a child will share her memories and give you
answers to your questions; answers that reflect the simplicity
and clarity of untouched minds–clear and simple.

It's my thinking, that at this age, they are too young to
fabricate much, because they don't know much, and not
old enough to have had all the other worldly feelings and
thoughts scrubbed out of them. What's more, they may not
have started school yet, so no one outside their families has
had the opportunity to influence what they believe. They are

still in the land of bedtime stories, and these make a lot of sense to them because they so often mirror the twinkling lights we call 'fairies', and other small light beings they may remember from the place they've recently left.

Rebecca had already shown an ability to see things that no one else in her family could. One morning, when she was about two years old, she identified her long deceased great-grandfather standing at the top of the kitchen stairs.

"Oh my God, Mom," Karen called me on the phone. "This morning Rebecca told me she saw Papa!"

When her mother told me this story, I was almost certain that she was remembering that time before she was born.

"How?" I asked. This was long before she had enough words to express herself with. She was just a baby. How had she identified my father—the man my children called 'Papa'?

Karen paused. "She was standing at the foot of the stairs and staring up at the landing—standing dead still, and then she pointed up the stairs. I asked her what she was looking at and she said, 'Papa'."

Karen took a deep breath. "Papa died years ago. Rebecca never knew him and I doubt she's ever heard his name!"

This was probably true. Her great-grandfather had lived in Europe and died long before she was born. At two years old it was highly unlikely, in my opinion, that she would have noted, or remembered, any casual remark about him within her family. Nobody has time to explain long-gone relatives to two year olds when you're changing diapers and chasing three young children around as Karen was doing.

"But listen to this . . ." she went on, "this is what's so weird. When I asked Rebecca what he looked like, she held her finger tips to her lips, running them back and forth, making the motions of someone playing a harmonica!"

Playing his harmonica was my father's favorite thing to do. He would pull out the instrument and play it whenever we were gathered as a family. Very often, when I was a child, we had makeshift bands, instigated by my father, usually after dinner. Someone played the piano, someone else sang, I was usually on drums, which involved a cardboard box and two wooden spoons, and friends might be given a saucepan or two to clash together as symbols. And of course, my dad was on his harmonica.

"Oh my God, Mom! For a moment I was so freaked out I didn't know what to do!" Karen said. "And then she pointed up the stairs and called him by name! None of us can ever remember talking to her about Papa!"

"Think it's possible she knew him on the Other Side?" I asked. "Before she was born?"

"You're getting weird on me . . ." I could hear one of her hooded stares in her tone. "Is that what you think?"

"Maybe." Heaven forbid that I weird her out.

"How else would she know? I hate to say it, but it's about the only thing that makes any sense." She said. "It's sooo weird!"

This was exciting. One day, I promised myself, I would ask Rebecca all of the questions that were swirling in my mind. But it was too soon. I wanted her to tell me as much as she knew, but first she was going to have to learn to speak.

~

It was two years later, when Rebecca was almost four, that I sat down beside her and started to engage her in the simplest and most direct way I could think of.

"Boo," I said, "Where were you before you were born? Do you remember the place you were in before you came here?"

She nodded and tucked her hair behind her ear.

"Will you tell me about it?"

She looked at me as though I had flipped. "I was in my mommy's tummy! Don't you know *that*, Mimi?" She spread her hands in disbelief and sighed.

Apparently I had not been direct enough.

"Yes, I know that Boo, but, what I want to know is, where were you before mommy's tummy?"

She paused, her eyelids lowered and then she said, "In a place." Silence. She was sitting beside me on the couch and she ran her hands down the sides of her legs pulling her dress down over her knees.

"Can you tell me about that place?"

She nodded. "It was big. An' pretty with flowers and cookies."

"Were there people there?"

44

Rebecca beamed and nodded and began to count off on her fingers. "Lots 'a people!"

"Did you know these people?"

"Yup!"

"Were they your friends?"

"Course! I love them—a lot" How can you be so dumb, Mimi, implied.

Her brother Brock, who was nearly seven years older than Rebecca, had come quietly into the room and was sitting on the floor listening. It struck me that this was totally out of character for a ten year old boy who normally would have been interrupting or standing on his head to get my attention. But he just sat there watching his sister.

"Brock," I asked. "Do you remember anything about the place you came from?"

"Yup. Same place."

I was stunned. He looked at me seriously. His thick brown hair was damp and his cheeks were pink. "There were cradles or something in this big room . . ." He stopped and frowned. "I can't remember much, but there were sleeping babies in them."

I waited. "Do you remember why they were there?"

"Nope. The light was kinda cloudy–like mist."

"Was it dark like nighttime or was it daylight?"

"No. It wasn't dark but it wasn't bright as day. It was sort of light . . . smooth–soft like air with colors . . ." He searched for words.

"What colors?"

"Blue and yellow! And I think it was making a sort of a sound like some kind of singing . . ." He nodded vigorously and brushed his hair back from his forehead. Then he burst into embarrassed laughter. "Ha, ha! I just told you a story! An' you b'lieved me! Ha, ha!"

I made a face at him. "What'd you do that for?"

"Jus' jokin'!"

~

I might have believed that except for the yellow and blue light. For a few moments, I knew that my grandson had let himself remember.

As a young child I remember cradling a handful of blue jacaranda flowers in my hand inhaling their scent, and feeling warm inside. It was the same feeling I used to get watching the puffy yellow weaver birds as they made their nests on the spindly branches of the tree outside my nursery window. That sense of yearning for something.

Are these some of the colors of that place we come from? Have you noticed how many people choose blues and yellows in their home decorating and in their gardens? Is it because they make us feel good? Or are we subconsciously reconstructing memories? Or maybe both. Surely, it's not a coincidence.

I turned back to Rebecca. "Did you see those colors, Boo?"

"Yup. An' cars and houses," she made a wide motion with her arms. "*Big* houses an' lights an' roads!"

"Really? There's a big city in the place you came from?"

"Nah uh. Nope." She shook her head. "I saw it through the hole."

"What hole?"

"*Mimi* you know!"

"I've forgotten–tell me." She obviously found me painfully slow.

"There's a hole," she said patiently, "An' you can see through it. Right down to James's house."

James was her younger cousin.

"Was he there? In one of those houses?"

Rebecca squealed with glee. "No, silly! He wasn't borned yet!"

"Rebecca . . ." That was Karen from the kitchen. "Don't be rude."

"Where was he?" I persisted.

"With *me*!"

"You and James were both looking through the hole in Heaven?"

She nodded.

"Why were you looking at those houses?"

"'Cos he said that's where he was going an' that's where I wanted to go too. I wanted to go with him when he got borned, but they said, 'No.'

The hairs were standing up on my arms. "Who said 'no'?

"Papa. He tol' me to go to *my* mommy not James's mom."

I was stunned.

"She's making that up, Mimi." Her brother remarked sternly.

She shook her head, "Na unh!"

I put my hand up. "Boo, do you know where James lives now?"

"Course! Noo York."

"Have you ever seen a picture of New York?"

"Nope. But I know what it looks like!"

"No, she doesn't." Her sibling muttered.

"Shhh." I said softly.

"I do too know what it looks like! I jus' told you!"

I was exhilarated. Both kids had given me a peek through the veil at the place they'd come from. Rebecca remembered at least two of the people who were there with her. No wonder she had recognized her great-grandfather 'Papa' when she could barely speak.

And my grandson, her brother, remembered the colors and the light. They both remembered.

~

Like Little Jackie Vapors, in Puff the Magic Dragon, Rebecca and her brother, got busy with the business of growing up and they put away the memories. At least I think they did. I never questioned her again but I listened to her dreams and we talked about them sometimes. We still do.

There was the dream she had not long after her Uncle Drew passed away. She was ten at the time. "It was so weird, Mimi." She told me. "I was with Uncle Drew and we were travelling all over the place. We were here at my house, we were at the lake house and we even went to New York.

Do you think he went with me to visit all the places we were in before he died?"

I nodded. "I think so."

"But the trouble was," she spread her hands, "No one in the dream could see him but me! I kept saying to everyone, "Uncle Drew's here! Look! It's Uncle Drew! And everyone just stared at me like they didn't know what I was talking about!"

I could feel her frustration.

"It was like I was the only one who could see him," she said. "Why, Mimi?"

"Maybe the others just aren't ready to see him yet," I told her.

"But why could I?"

"Do you think he knows you can see him, so he picked you to tell everyone else that he was there?"

"Yup. Maybe–know *I* saw him."

"I know you did too." I wanted her to know that it was okay to share those dreams and to wonder, and to ask questions and draw her own conclusions.

Five years later, when Rebecca was fifteen, she and I drove to South Carolina together. My son Michael had invited us all down to his house near Georgetown for a week at the beach.

It was seven a.m. on July 21st, and the morning was already warm. The sun had been up for an hour or more when we left my house for the start of the six hour journey, but it was much too early for Rebecca who had been up late the night before. As we cruised down the driveway she tilted the seat back, wrapped herself in a beach towel and closed her eyes for a snooze.

"I'll wake you up when we get to Greensboro," I told her, "and you can help navigate our way onto Interstate 40." The interchange was confusing enough without commuter traffic but this morning we would be arriving smack in the middle of morning rush hour and two heads are always better than one when you're trying to read exit signs that flash by at 65 miles an hour.

"Okay, Mimi." I heard her sleepy voice from somewhere under the towel and put my hand out to pat her.

It was a strange morning. From the time I began packing the car for our trip and again in the moment we left the house, I'd had the feeling that we weren't alone. I'd felt Drew outside the car and then again as I settled down and started the engine. It didn't surprise me. That day would have been his birthday.

I wondered if Rebecca still had dreams of him . . . or if she was even open to those feelings of hers anymore. Would she still share those dreams if I asked her, I wondered. Should I tell her that Drew was here?

Expecting nothing more than a rumble out of her I said, "Uncle Drew's driving with us. I have the strongest feeling that he's in the car with us."

Nothing. Then a sleepy grunt. I waited and decided to push my luck. "Just wait, I'm getting the feeling that he's going to play one of his favorite songs for us on the radio—we'll hear it somewhere between here and Georgetown." I knew a handful of Drew's songs and I knew she was listening. "I think it will be Nickleback's *"Photograph."* That was one of his favorites." A barely audible grunt came from under a tangle of sun-bleached hair and red and yellow beach towel.

The road through the foothills of the Blue Ridge was like a roller coaster in places; up hills and down dales. Tall

Eastern hard woods, old cedars and oak crowded the roadside and small towns appeared suddenly and vanished just as quickly behind us. Traffic was light, except for a dozen or so big trucks and a sprinkling of cars and pickup trucks, and we were cruising along through the early morning hills, still purple with dawn and damp with dew. Ancient mountains that were born eons ago–kicked up tall, jagged and smoking by giant upheavals and mammoth quakes in the earth's crust. The spine of the Appalachian chain that was once taller than the Rockies, has been swallowed by the earth and regurgitated multiple times, leaving us with the now with gently rounded peaks, sweeping green valleys and grassy meadows.

Two hours later, with Rebecca asleep beside me, we left the countryside behind and entered the outskirts of Greensboro in North Carolina where Route 220 merges into the traffic on Route 68. Commuter traffic was moving well as I eased the car into the stream of vehicles. Leaning across the console, I shook Rebecca's shoulder. "Wake up, Boo, be my navigator. I'm going to need your help in a few minutes."

She stirred.

The closer we got to the city, the airport and Interstate 40, the more crowded the roads became and the faster the traffic moved. City and airport commuters, as well as beach-goers like ourselves drove fast and furiously southward. I gripped the steering wheel feeling the tension rise as the unfamiliar intersection and transition from 68 to Interstate 40 raced to meet us. My eyes were glued to the road, all my concentration was on staying in my lane and not getting side-swiped by someone in a bigger hurry than I was. The big green interstate signs loomed above us on each side of the inky black freeway, cars and trucks roared by, spinning onto the exit ramps, roaring ahead of us from the entrance ramps.

Rebecca was awake and sitting up, her eyes fixed on the signs and exit numbers as we raced by. The air was tense around me, my hands clutched the steering wheel in a death-like grip, my jaw ached from my clenched teeth and I was hardly breathing when I felt a tap on my knee and heard, "Listen, Mimi–Nickleback." I spun into our exit. "They're playing *'Photograph.'*"

Yes, they were. I beamed at Rebecca and let out a deep breath. "Told you–Uncle Drew's here. Did you know that it's his birthday today?"

Soon we were back in the wide open countryside again with miles and miles of straight road stretching ahead of us. I could breathe again and Rebecca grinned. "Yup. I was waiting for it–and it happened! You were right, Mimi. Can I go back to sleep now?"

"Sweet dreams, Boo."

Rebecca's sixth sense was alive and well and I was pleased, thinking that it probably wouldn't be lost in the chaotic crunch of her teenage world, her sports and all the drama of high school. With any luck she'd hold onto it for life.

Later that evening, when the children were gathered in the living room of the beach house playing cards, I overheard her talking to her cousin James.

"It was so weird–Mimi said, just wait, we're going to hear that song that Uncle Drew liked–*'Photograph'*. You know that song?"

James nodded.

"Well, it was just like she said–about halfway there it started playing on the radio in the car!" She began to hum the tune.

James chimed in with the lyric then stopped abruptly, his eyes lit up and I heard him say, "And that's not the only weird thing . . . last night, on the last night of camp, they had a talent contest and one kid got up and began to sing that very song *'Photograph'*! He was so good! It was awesome and everyone was shouting and clapping. Man– he sounded just like those guys!"

He and Rebecca began to sing. "I didn't know Uncle Drew knew that song," James said.

Drew was at the beach with us. He'd been with us in the car and with James on the last night of camp. How totally cool! How amazingly fantastic!

Chapter 7: Twins

"He came here for a reason."

This is the twin's story. One baby boy was a lively seven pounder, the other, at barely five pounds, was born a very sick little person, with a congenital heart defect. The parents were told that they could expect their child would live a restricted life dominated by hospital admissions and the chronic implications of his diseased heart. The prognosis for a life beyond these critical first two months was not hopeful.

As it turned out, modern medicine was able to give him many more days and weeks than they had predicted but his health was never good and, with every week of his young life, it got worse. It reached a crisis point late one night when the baby was eleven months old and had to be rushed by ambulance into the O.R. for a last ditch open-heart surgery, in a desperate attempt to save his life.

It wasn't to be.

~

It wasn't as though this turn for the very worst was unexpected, but people talked about how no one was ever prepared for the news of a baby's death. They shared insights about what it meant; thinking about how sad the family was–the tragedy they would live with from now on, and how devastating it was that he had died so young. Eventually, people went their separate ways and got on with the business of living their own lives.

When I got the news, I went for a walk. Walking is good. It's especially good when you're grappling with questions you can't find the answers to. Why are babies born only to die less than a year later? It wasn't fair! If something good is supposed to come out of something bad, I have to ask, what good can come out of something so harsh? But walking is good. And the faster I walked the faster, it seemed, I could move away from the incomprehensible craziness of life. The frustration I felt didn't go away, but the surge of warm blood racing to the surface of my skin, flushing it pink, dampening my hair, was good. It made me feel the fact of my own continual survival, and for that moment it was okay.

It was a brisk morning, brisker than I'd bargained for when I slung my jacket over the dining room chair, and gone out without it. So I fixed my mind firmly on the shortest route home, and picked up the pace.

The only time I broke stride was to bend down and lace my shoe; and that was when it happened. It was like a bird flying in my face. A rush of warm energy. It came so suddenly that my breath caught in my chest as I stood up leaving the shoe half-laced. I stood very still feeling something like a deer in the woods when he senses something near. 'What was that?' No sooner had the thought escaped when I got the clear mental image of a baby.

A healthy baby toddled towards me on unsteady chubby legs dragging a stuffed animal. And then a thought, as solid as the earth in summer, but as gentle as the first snow flakes, flew through my mind, leaving behind its indelible meaning on the limited receptors of my human brain. I wanted to say 'loud and clear'–but there was no sound. Only the undeniable imprint of its intent.

"He came here for a reason." I heard. "You're asking yourself; why did this have to happen to our particular family? Did they do something wrong? Are they being punished?

The truth is that our family is one of the best of families. There is real love in our home. Our parents love each other and adore us. They care for one another, and they care for others too. People like them. In fact everyone is drawn to them for the positivity they bring to the community. There are lots of friends too.

So why them? You ask. Here's where it gets tricky," I heard. "Sometimes Heaven's very best ambassadors choose a life of sacrifice and tragedy to help others see the things that are important. Take Magic Johnson—big star, a beacon of light and achievement who had the talent and the ability to reach millions of people. Look what happened! He was struck down by Aids for the whole world to see. But it doesn't matter whether you reach millions or just those in your community. The idea is to help souls to evolve."

Could it be that this sick baby boy who was born, and left so quickly, came in to pull his community together? To help people realize what's important; that the love and support of each other means everything and that the community of friends is an essential part of our well-being. Not who's got the biggest house on the block or whose son just got accepted to Harvard, or who built the biggest swimming pool in the neighborhood.

Rather, did the baby's passing make families hold each other tighter before they went to bed that night? Did they draw on the love they had for each other, and make more time to be there for each other; leaning on one other in a time of crisis, in an effort to become one loving family with the family who lost their baby? Was it for their own family's good? Or could it have been for the community? Maybe it was it part of some overall big plan that was put together in some distant dimension, for the evolvement of humanity? One day we'll know.

But who was that talking to me? The message was clear and very sure. Then I knew exactly who was out there walking with me, grabbing my attention. That warm push of energy, right in my face, belonged to the sick baby's twin. Suddenly I was sure. That initial image of the toddler—it was the well baby. I knew what I was hearing. It was the well baby's spirit speaking to my spirit. The well baby's spirit had travelled to where I was to let me know it had something to say and it wanted to be heard.

Something else the neighborhood friend had said when she called, was how great it was that so many old friends had come together over this baby's illness. People who hadn't seen each other for years, gathered together doing whatever they could for the broken family. Messages of support poured in and they were surrounded by the love of people from near and far.

"Funny how something like this makes you realize that we're all in this together," my friend observed. "Like an ear-ringing wake-up call."

It may have been a reminder to all of us that we are all One. This could have been any of us. And that uneasy thought brought us all together, pooling our strength for each other.

That was the message. *People matter.* Possessions are nothing but fancy trappings; that, in the light of real loss seem so unimportant. It's people who are everything. And when we realize that, we all join hands to pull each other through; a community of family, friends and strangers. This time, this loving family, who had lost so much, was our teacher.

~

I think that with Magic, the awareness of the early AIDS epidemic was shoved front and center into the hearts and minds of all of us as we came face to face with what became a worldwide tragedy—that could have happened in our own families; and so many of us went to work to find a cure, to show compassion and yes, be humbled, knowing that tragedy strikes even the brightest and strongest of us.

~

That by itself, would have been enough to convince me of why this baby had been born. But, half way through my walk, thinking of nothing in particular, another image slammed into view. Again, it caught me teetering on my left f o o t–unawares.

There in front of me was the vision of a very light and airy, almost translucent place. It was like a picture with fuzzy edges, soft and feathered, and inside the picture was the image of a young man. He was laughing, shaking hands with people, greeting friends and family. It looked as though he had recently returned from a trip to some distant place. Happiness, joy and a feeling of love, unlike anything we have on earth, filled the space of this reunion making it feel like a sunny day in January.

I knew immediately that I was looking at the sick baby who had passed in surgery. This was him, in spirit, at the perfect age, back home again in Heaven. His thoughts came through to me very clearly, crossing dimensions smoothly, with no barriers, making me feel as though I was looking across the room and listening to someone else's conversation.

"Wow! That was a hard one!" He smiled and put his hands on his hips, shaking his head. And I knew he meant his short, painful life and the sadness he had left on earth.

The vision was clear but fleeting and then, to further rock my boat, I turned my head and noticed that standing behind him, with his arms crossed in front of him, enjoying everything that was happening, was the well twin's spirit. There was a wide smile on his face as he watched his brother's home-coming. He was free of disease and pain, free of the ties that held him for the short time he spent on earth. The twins were both in spirit, both the same age, and I 'heard' the well baby say, "I came over with him–just to be with him one more time. I'll be leaving now." And with that, he raised his hand in farewell, his brother turned around and returned the acknowledgement, and the vision was gone.

~

You may ask why this toddler's spirit chose to speak to me instead of someone closer to him. Here's what I think: The surviving twin's spirit was aware of the deep tragedy that permeated his immediate world when his brother passed. He could feel the anguish and sorrow, not only in his family but in the community and I believe he wanted to help by showing us the bigger picture.

His parents were immersed in grief for his brother and themselves. The vibration around them was like heavy wet cotton making it difficult for a spirit of a much higher and lighter vibration to breach. There was no getting through to them. So, he decided to try another route and that's when he found me on my solitary walk. My mind was tuned in, my vibration was engaged but unencumbered, my spirit was available to talk and there were no distractions. It was much easier to reach me than any of his close family members. So he did and I became his messenger.

I have a feeling this child, this spiritual being, will make himself heard and felt in many more ways over his lifetime. As he gets older, he'll be the little boy in the playground who stops to pick up a clumsy friend who's fallen down in the race. He'll be the one who shares his lunch with someone who has none. He'll be the one who comforts others. He's what we call an empath.

Chapter 8: Adam

". . . there was this 'splosion—an' all the bildin's fell down."

"It was about a week ago," Joy emailed me. "Such a beautiful day, I couldn't bear to stay inside so I got my gardening tools and went into the garden. I remember noticing how blue the sky was, and so clear. As I watched, an airplane flew over and I know if it had been any closer I could have seen the people inside it."

Enjoying the sunshine on her face and the tingling of warmth on her bare arms, Joy stayed outside for a long time pulling weeds and dead-heading old roses. Even when she got tired, she couldn't bear the thought of leaving her garden and the sunny day, so instead of going inside, she made her way to the porch swing on the verandah and eased herself down among the cushions. She stared out at the newly-weeded and pruned garden, pleased with her handiwork.

Some new neighbors had just moved in next door and she noticed a young boy playing by himself in their front yard. "It made me wish my children were still little and out digging in the dirt, but they're all grown now," she said wistfully. "Then he looked up and I waved to him and said, 'Hi' and he waved back."

She saw him a couple of times after that and one day he wandered across the lawn to the porch and asked if he could swing.

It was another blue sky day and Joy was in no hurry to go in. "I had met his mother by now, so I said, "Sure!" and moved over to make room. I asked him his name."

"Adam." He replied.

"Where are you from, Adam?"

He didn't know, so she asked, "Did you move from somewhere close by?"

He shook his head. "No. I lived far away in a big place with big buildin's and a lotta cars. B*rrooom . . . broom!*" He paused, rubbed his grubby hands on his shorts and tilted his head back. "Lookit that plane up there!" He suddenly said hanging onto the arm of the swing and pointing at the sky.

"We see a lot of those here," Joy told him. "They fly right over us on their way to the airport." She shaded her eyes and watched a commercial jet climbing fast and high as it took off for who knows where.

"Is it going to crash us?" The child asked.

Joy laughed and shook her head. "Good Lord, I hope not! Why would you think that?"

"'Cos once it did–*Wham!*" His small hands smacked together in a loud clap. "*Wham! Bang!*" he shouted holding his hands high, watching the airplane and its con trail as it disappeared from view.

Joy was taken aback. "I don't think so," she laughed, but then noticed how serious the child's face was, and said, "It did?"

"Yup."

"Then what happened?"

"There was a giant *'splosion!* An' all the bildin's fell down." He drew his shoulders in towards his chest and ducked his head covering it with his hands.

"And you saw all that?" That wasn't good! Joy was alarmed. "After that, what happened?"

He was quiet, shaking his head, staring far into the distance. "Nothin'."

Joy found out later that the family had never lived in a big city where planes crashed into buildings, toppling them to the ground. His mother confided to her that the little boy's imagination sometimes got out of hand, although, for some reason, he did seem to be leery of air planes flying over. "Ever since he was little he would point at them and make anxious noises." She apologized and said she would speak to him about telling such stories.

"I wanted to tell her 'No! Ask him what else he saw that day!' Because it suddenly struck me that maybe he wasn't imagining things or telling stories. I wondered if he was remembering a past life. And then I thought, Oh my God! Was it a memory of a life in New York City? A memory of September 11th when the twin towers came down?"

Joy did follow up the conversation with the boy's mother who said, she was certain he had never heard of that terrible day, or the planes crashing, or the buildings coming down. "He wasn't even born when it happened!"

She exclaimed. "And who in their right mind would tell a young child about that day. . . I don't understand it."

"It was 2007 when he told me that story," Joy told me. "He was four years old and the terrorist attack in New York happened three years before he was born."

~

Could it be a memory of another life? The believers and researchers of reincarnation believe that people who die violent deaths often come back into this world very quickly, to finish up a lifetime cut short. Was it possible that this child was one of the people who had died in the 9/11 attack?

Dr Ian Stevenson, a former head of The University of Virginia's Psychology department might have thought so.

Stevenson, now deceased, was considered to be the world's foremost authority on reincarnation and by the time he died, he had documented over three thousand five hundred accounts of past lives, taken from young children from around the world.

The children came from both Western and Eastern cultures whose philosophies regarding reincarnation are quite different, and the study was, in part, to find out whether those cultures had any influence on the answers the children gave him. What he discovered in the course of his study was that their stories about past lives were strikingly consistent, no matter which side of the globe they came from. So, it could be concluded that religion, custom, culture and philosophy played no part in their memories; memories that could very often be verified by family members, old birth records, headstones and dates.

These were the soul memories that the children brought with them into a new life on earth. Memories that they were willing to share before someone told them to pipe down. Was the child who came to live next door to Joy one of those children whose recall of a past life was still etched on his memory?

I have no trouble thinking that the imprinting of such an act of unimaginable and horrific violence might very easily have survived his physical life, his transition, and be brought back into a future incarnation. What do you think?

~

It happens to many of us. How many times have you walked down a strange street and had the sudden thought, "I know this street!" The problem is, you have no memory of ever having seen it before. At least not in this lifetime.

72

Whenever I set about trying to prove or disprove something, my rule of thumb is to approach it with skepticism, and question everything about it. If I can rule out the possibility that it looks similar to another street I know well, and if I can verify that I've never been anywhere near this particular street before, it could be a flash of recognition of a past life.

It's always tempting to be over-enthusiastic and willing to believe anything because we really, really want to. But if you want to know the truth, in so far as it's possible to do so, then it's better to eliminate any possibility that it is *not* reincarnation. Once you can do that, you're left with the only thing that makes any sense which is the probability of a past life experience.

Children's life experiences are limited, and that is one of many reasons why they are used in any serious study of reincarnation. There is no experience in this present life that might suggest themes for their stories of past lives. They just don't know enough to make up complicated stories with details that are remarkable to say the least. For instance, how can a three year old, living in Florida, give you a vivid picture of an avalanche in Washington State that happened a hundred years ago? That happened, and there are hundreds of other 'unexplainable' accounts of similar happenings.

...as it is in Heaven

Chapter 9: Jennifer

"How do you know there's a park around the corner?"

Many adults retain memories of childhood experiences of pre-existence too.

Take Jennifer for example, who clearly remembers her early childhood in Virginia and North Carolina, and the memories she had of past life experiences.

"Summer time was the most fun time," she said. "My family would take a trip nearly every summer after school was out. These trips were nothing spectacular, but to my sister and me they were like circuses, Disney and County Fairs all rolled in one! We got so excited we could hardly stand it as we listened to plans being made around were we were going this time, and who we might see."

Sometimes it would be a trip to beach, sometimes to the mountains, sometimes to visit relatives for family reunions.

"It didn't matter where we went," Jennifer said, "we loved them all, and the people who were there–whether, as children, we knew anyone or not. I especially loved the pecan pies and hush puppies one of the Aunts brought from Louisiana. They were good times." Her eyes sparkled as she told the story.

"But long before I was able to understand anything about going to the beach or the mountains, State Parks or anything, I have these memories I've never been able to forget," she went on. "I must have been very young on some of these travels, and there were many times when I remember telling my mother and father about sights and happenings around the next corner, or what we would see ahead. None of these were spectacular either, they were just ordinary things; like once I remember telling them, 'There's a white church around this corner, or a red house . . . or children on a swing in a park." Jennifer said. "It happened over and over, and you should have seen their faces when we rounded the corner and there right in front of us was a red house or a white church with children on a playground swing."

"How did you know that?" A parent would ask in disbelief. And I would just shrug. I didn't know how I knew that–I just knew.

It happened many times, Jennifer said. "Once I told them about a bridge up ahead with shaky rails. And cheerfully sang out to 'Be careful—there's a train down there!' And sure enough, before long, we'd come to a railroad crossing. I don't remember if there was a train or not, but you get the point.

There was no way I could have known about any of this. Most of these were new places that none of us had ever seen before, and even with the family visits, I would hardly have remembered being taken there as a tiny baby, would I?"

Probably not. But who knows for sure what tiny brains retain? Anything is possible, but these memories that made such an impression on Jennifer, combined with the verification of her parents that they had never been to these places before, makes reincarnation the most likely conclusion. It sounds to me as though they were clear memories of a place where she had probably lived in a not-too-distant past life.

As Jennifer got older, she mostly just stored these strange memories away until many years later, when there was another tweak from the Universe.

"We were living in Norfolk, Virginia at the time, and belonged to the neighborhood Methodist church. As it is with many churches, we had an exchange situation with another Methodist church in Norfolk. This one was on the other side of the city. The way the exchange worked was that the preachers and choir from the other church came to our church for Sunday services for a month, and we switched and our preacher and choir went to theirs.

On the last week of the exchange, the other church invited the members from our church to join them for a pot luck dinner. I guess most of our members weren't in a travelling mood so only a couple of carloads made the trip across town. I was in one of the groups that accepted the church's invitation to dinner.

"As we drove through the gates," she said, "We were greeted by the sight of an old, stone church, with the most beautiful stained glass windows.

We went inside to be shown around, and it was obvious to me that the church was very old indeed. It's darkly polished wooden pews, shiny and pitted with age old scars and grooves told of many hundreds of people who had worshipped here at one time or another. When I looked down at the concrete floor, I could see worn places where hundreds of feet had trodden."

Jennifer said the church just had a *feeling* about it. "It seemed as though I knew this place," she said. "I can't explain it, but it felt very comfortable. So, when dinner was over, I got up from the table and wandered into the sanctuary of the old church and felt as though I was being led to sit down in one of the pews. So, I did."

Jennifer smiled as she told the story. "I remember sitting there very quietly, almost in awe, staring at the tall stained-glass windows in brilliant colors surrounding the sanctuary, and felt my eyes drawn to an old pipe organ in a prominent place at the front of the church. It was so peaceful there, I could have sat there forever in the solitude and comfort of the old church. For some strange reason, I felt as though I belonged there and when it was time to go, it was difficult to leave."

But leave she did, and was very quiet on the ride home, still caught up in the spell of the stone church.

"Not long after that, I had a chance to talk to my father about it. I asked him what he knew about it, if he had ever been inside."

"Well," he tossed his head back and laughed. He seemed to be remembering something. He was quiet for a moment and then he said, 'Your mother and I were married in that old church.'

Well! I had never known that! And then he said, 'Matter of fact, you were christened there too.' I was stunned. I had been in this church before!

But how on earth would I have remembered that as a tiny baby? That's impossible! But wait, is that why I felt so comfortable there?"

~

And I say, it could be that, or what if, it's a pre-existence memory? What if Jennifer was on the Other Side when she first 'met' her new earth parents? Perhaps she was in the middle of making a decision to come back to earth and was wondering what sort of parents she should pick. Is it possible she was watching their wedding taking place in that old stone church—did someone guide her to that sunny day in North Carolina? One of her guides perhaps?

Perhaps Jennifer took one look and fell in love with the man and woman who were exchanging vows that day, and then and there, decided she would be born to them one day in the not too distant future.

Or maybe that baby girl lay in her godmother's arms on the day of her christening, just taking in all the beauty of the sunlight shining through the brightly stained glass windows, smiling at all the happy faces around her on the day she was christened. That would be a memory to keep, I think.

Who knows what those tiny brains are capable of?

Chapter 10: Pre-birth Visits from the Other Side

"Holly! That's a nice name for a girl!" Where did that come from?

I am convinced that most, if not all children, remember where they've come from and that their memories can, and often do, point the way to a pre-birth existence.

How do you know that, Ginny?

I'm glad you asked. I know that because very often, people, especially expectant mothers, "hear" from their babies before birth. Some have seen them before they are born, in dreams, or in a flash of intuition.

Sometimes, you'll hear one of these mothers say, "I'm sure it's a girl." Or a boy, as the case may be. It's just a feeling that she has and it's usually right. And sometimes it's more than just a feeling. Sometimes the baby will appear in a dream she has, or she'll begin to feel, on some unknown level, that she not only knows it's a boy, but she knows what the child looks like, and what sort of personality it has.

An outsider might be tempted to believe that she's just guessing, And that's always a possibility, but when the mother has a deep 'knowingness' that she's right, then it's much more than a guess. I believe it's the mother's spirit tweaking her, saying, "Look, I'm in touch with the baby's spirit, who, by the way, has chosen to be a boy this time around. We talk a lot, and here's what he's like."

Other people in and outside the mother's circle have sometimes been known to pick up the sex of the unborn child too. And it has nothing to do with the shape of the bulge, or the way the mother carries a baby, or what her cravings happen to be, or any number of other old wives' observations. Not to put down folk lore, but there's something much stronger and surer at work with some mothers-to-be. Some call it intuition.

What I'm talking about is a strong spirit connection with the incoming spirit that is clear and accurate and needs no guesswork. It's always there but very often, the mother is not aware of that connection. It could be that she's too busy to think about it, caring for other children, working a job, or just plain tired. But I'm willing to bet that at some time during the pregnancy most mothers will be given a tweak by the new spirit that's coming in. It might be in a dream or simply a passing thought or a flower that catches her eye. Or, for no reason at all she may think, "Holly! That's a pretty name for a girl. It's cute. Strange, I've never thought of that before!"

Maybe it was a tweak from the new, soon to be small human, who wanted that name for this life time?

"But 'Holly'?" her mom-to-be says. "She's not due until late January!"

Well, guess what, Baby Holly might also be nudging you to let you know that she'll be here early–maybe on Christmas Eve; or Christmas Day or the week before or after Christmas. You just never know.

Awareness with a capital A is everything.

If I'm talking about you, if you've ever wondered if your baby is listening to you, listening to your plans for him or her, you're right. We already know that they can hear voices and music while they're in utero. What if the soon-to-be incarnated spirit is listening carefully, not snoozing, and wanting to give his opinion? I hope you'll stay aware during the pregnancy and that you won't push the tweaks away. Don't shrug them off. Take a chance, and allow yourself to think, that just maybe it's more than a whim, more than imagination or coincidence that this baby likes the name 'Holly'.

Allow yourself to wonder. You don't need a psychic or an old wife to tell you what the baby's going to be. Every one of us has the ability to connect with the Sixth Sense, but not everyone knows how to use it or has it to the same degree as some others. It's very like the physical senses. Some may have more sensitivity in their finger tips, than others. Others may see or hear better than most. And, as with our god-given gifts, one person may become an Olympic swimmer while another can't even get the hang of a half-way efficient dog-paddle.

You can even indulge in a tool or two to help you find out more about the tiny being you're carrying. We were divining the sex of babies for fun, long before the age of sonograms. Have you ever dangled a ring, a pendulum, or a wishbone, over a pregnant woman's abdomen, and depending on which way it swings, you try to discover the sex of the unborn child? That's one of the tools of divination that people sometimes use. It's like using a crystal ball for fortune telling. But, in actual fact, we all have an innate ability to access our Sixth Sense. We don't need any crystal balls or wishbones.

~

Here's what I mean: The first time an unborn baby made herself known to me, was in a dream. In the dream, I was in my daughter Karen's house, standing inside the sliding glass doors, looking out onto a small, square deck where her two young children played in a sand box. They were three and four years old at the time.

As I watched them, I noticed that there was a third child in the sandbox with them. It was a little girl, sitting with her back to me, wearing a pale yellow sundress with a tiny floral design. She had her back to me and her legs were folded underneath her. I didn't recognize her, but I somehow knew she was connected to the other children. The child was a toddler of two or three years old, with strawberry blonde hair, and as I watched her, she turned, looked me straight in the eye and gave me a smile that could light up midnight. Then she was gone and I woke up.

Who was the child? I spent the better part of that day wondering if it was one of their friends I may have seen at a birthday party, or from the playgroup they attended. And I kept drawing blanks. But somehow I just knew she was connected to my two grandchildren.

And then a thought landed plop in my lap. Was Karen expecting another baby? Karen hadn't even hinted at anything like that. Was this a new spirit coming in to their family? The dream intrigued me. It had me guessing so, by late afternoon, I picked up the phone and teasingly asked Karen if she was hiding something from me.

"I had this dream," I told her and I can't figure out who the little girl in the sand box was, but I knew she was part of your family."

"Well, stop dreaming, Mom! There is *no* third baby anywhere on the horizon! When would I have time to look after it? One of my existing kids hasn't had his nose wiped in two days, the other's run out of socks because there's a basket full of wash on the kitchen floor waiting to be washed, and there is a trail of toilet paper running down the stairs because one of them got tired of sitting on the potty and decided to finish the job unassisted, leaving a trail of . . .

"*Okay*, stop! I get it!" I was laughing now. "Just let me tell you what I saw."

"You've got two minutes. That's when the plumber gets here to unplug the guest bathroom because there's a shoe flushed down the toilet. Just to see where it would go".

"She's beautiful." I said quietly. "Pink and white complexion, strawberry blonde hair framing a round face, and the most fabulous smile you've ever seen."

"That's lovely Mom," Karen pushed a stray hair back from her cheek and sighed. "Keep dreaming, but it's not going to happen."

Well, as we've all heard, life happens while we're making other plans and Rebecca was born two years later. And when she turned three, I found myself looking at the same chubby cheeked, strawberry blonde I'd met in my dream. With a smile that could stop a train.

~

From time to time, I've noticed, the future will creep into the present, giving you a glimpse of what's to come. The past does the same thing, only backwards.

We've been told by Einstein, and others with minds far greater than most, that there is no linear time in space, or beyond our earth. It's a difficult concept to grasp to say the least, but it does seem to jive with the teachings of spirituality, that the past, present and future are all happening simultaneously.

It's always interesting to me that along with much speculation about his incredible intellect, the one that resonates with many is that Einstein was a mystic. There are even those who have thought that he was channeling mathematical information from a higher source. He is also reported to have said that the concept of reincarnation is the only thing that made any sense to him. Perhaps this is why past, present and future events, stretching far beyond and before our time, can be channeled by present day psychics. They're all happening simultaneously. I think I would have liked Einstein.

Nostra Damas and Da Vinci did the same thing. One channeled events that would occur in the future, most popularly, political events, and the other, anatomical information far beyond his time.

~

Sometimes these glimpses of past and future events will come to us in dreams. They arrive during that quiet time when the conscious mind is still asleep and awareness is just on the edge of tweaking itself awake. In this down time between waking and sleeping, when there is no interference from the waking mind, with awareness sharp and unobstructed, beings from other dimensions are able to come through the veil without resistance. That resistance being The Mind, that for the time being is silenced, not jumping to conclusions or making assumptions or judgments of any kind.

Occasionally, you'll have a dream that is so real that you know it cannot possibly be a dream. You'll find that you won't need to convince yourself or anyone else about this dream. You just know it's a visit, not a dream. That's how I met Rebecca in her pre-existence state.

Rebecca is as intuitive as a cat. Her sixth sense is strong and, because no one's tried to shoo it away, it's been able to develop the way it can when it's left alone. She sees spirits and talks to them, and we've learned to listen when she's telling us about that part of a world that most of us have forgotten

Chapter 11: Jake, Alexandra and Charlie

"Here I come! Look at me!"

Someone close to me has a little boy named Jake. He's a quiet, serious little blonde, who popped into a forerunner dream I had before he was born. In fact, he came into that dream before his parents had shared the news with anyone else. In the dream, he looked as though he was about two years old. I believe that he just stopped by one night to let me know, "I'm on my way, this is me. And here's what I'll look like." It was just a fragment of a dream, but very clear, and I knew exactly who he was, and who his parents would be.

This is spirit communication. It was his soul talking to mine from the Other Side. As it turned out, this dream was a real blessing, and I remembered it at a time when we needed all the hope we could find, late on the night he was born.

His mother, Tessa, went into labor in the early morning. Nothing seemed to be moving much. Labor started, and then it stopped, and then it started again. It had turned into a very long day and by nine that night we were all getting anxious and praying for this to be over. Tessa is a small girl, this was a first baby and she was becoming exhausted. She had been struggling to give birth all day, but it seemed that her son just wasn't in a rush to be born.

Three hours later, with both mother and baby now in trouble, they used forceps to deliver him. We held our breath waiting for his first cry. It didn't come. Then we heard his mother cry out, *"He's stillborn! Oh my God—he's stillborn . . .*

The baby wasn't breathing. We watched as, in slow motion, the pediatrician and nursing staff took him from her and had him on the neo-natal crash cart wheeling him at top speed down the hallway into the nursery where he could be helped.

The baby's grandparents were standing near the nurses' station and caught their first glimpse of their tiny grandson, pale and inert, as they wheeled past, yelling at people to stand back.

Luke, the new baby's father, followed the cart leaving his wife with her doctor and her parents.

It seemed to take hours as they hooked the infant to machines, massaged his chest and rubbed his legs to stimulate him, trying to get him to breathe. Three nurses kept up the strokes, the gentle massage, turning the baby this way and that, trying everything get the baby to breathe.

All that time, his dad stood in front of the nursery window watching silently. He looked so alone. I walked over and stood beside him and together we watched the activity behind the glass. Medical people were coming and going. A cart stood beside the bassinette covered with a variety of instruments, pumps and tubing. One nurse was speaking rapidly into a wall telephone and another stood at the bottom of the cradle massaging both his tiny feet.

"I feel as though I'm watching my son die . . ." Luke whispered. His eyes were filling with tears and so were mine. The baby was a frightening bloodless gray color.

I turned away to hide my fear, and, as I did so, I remembered that flash dream I'd had long before this baby was born. When I turned back, I put my hand on the young man's arm. "The only thing I can tell you," I said, "and you can take it or leave it, but I saw this little guy in a dream–as healthy as can be, at the age of two."

There was silence between us. He stood with his hands in his pockets staring at the scene inside the nursery. "Okay." He said, so quietly I could hardly hear him.

"He's going to be okay," I said, hoping to God I was right. "Does his color look a little better to you?"

"Look! I think he's breathing!" Luke exhaled loudly. *"Thank God."* The baby was making thin, small sounds. He was breathing and alive.

That was the night I learned to trust those dreams.

Jake is a young man now. At 15 he is very blonde, serious and mostly quiet and studious with a gentle sense of humor. Just like the little boy I saw in the dream. He's a book worm, and I have a hunch that one day he'll read these stories I write and he'll wonder about them, and perhaps his own brain will take the research a step further into that other reality and other dimensions.

~

About two years after Jake was born I began having dreams of a little girl, as blithe and light as a pixie with curly light auburn hair, fair skin and a mischievous grin. She always showed up in white or pale yellow dresses with old fashioned puff sleeves. She seemed to skip wherever she went, and in more than one such dream I saw her with an old lady friend of mine named Laura Lee Brown.

In the dreams Laura Lee was a young woman, not the lovely old lady I knew now, who was over eighty years old, and in my dream, she and the child held hands while the little girl skipped across a lawn towards a big white house with a wrap-around verandah and a porch swing. In one of the dreams I'd seen the little girl swinging with Laura Lee sitting beside her.

The picture they made looked like something that had been painted by a French Impressionist artist in ethereal pastels, flecked in feathery white, bathed in misty light. But instead of a European garden, these dreams took place on the long, sweeping lawns of a southern mansion.

I didn't think much about them at the time because, to begin with, I had no idea who the child might be or who she belonged to–just that she seemed to have something to do with Laura Lee who had auburn hair that was just as red at eighty as it had been when she was much, much younger. With no help from Clairol, she swore.

Tessa and Luke, Jakes mom and dad, weren't even married when I had the first dream of Alexandra. They were in college at the time if I remember rightly. But, the years went by quickly, and in what seemed like a blink of an eye, they graduated, got married, got busy working and buying a house and getting on with their new lives. And then it was time for Jake to be born.

~

Several years after Jake's birth, I had a dream that Tessa was expecting her second baby and in that dream I was given a very clear picture of a chubby little boy with curly hair at the age of about two.

"No, I'm not," she said when I told her about my dream.

Then four months later, when I saw them again, Tessa announced that she was three months pregnant.

I knew it! I wanted to say, but I didn't. Neither did I say that I had seen the baby and it was definitely a boy.

When I asked them if they were going to find out whether the baby was a boy or a girl, they said "No." Neither parent wanted to know.

"It's more exciting this way," Tessa said. "It actually makes shopping more fun because you don't have to think inside the pink and blue boxes for girls or boys–you can pick out anything you like.

And then she asked, "What do you think this baby is, Ginny?"

"I'm not telling you," I grinned at her, "Don't want to ruin the surprise."

"Well, I think it's a girl," she said with a knowing little grin on her face.

"Hmmm," I said. "Funny. I got the image of a baby boy in that dream I told you about." I said tentatively

She nodded. "I know, but I just have the feeling that it's a girl."

"Then it probably is," I said.

I was confused. Not drastically so, because these things have a way of playing out, but mildly confused nevertheless. I had seen a boy. But I was also sure that this baby's mother had a much closer connection than I did, so she was undoubtedly right. But who was the baby boy I'd seen? I racked my brains for people I knew of who were pregnant, but could only think of one and she already knew she was having a girl. So, I let it be.

A new baby's spirit is closely and spiritually linked to its mother and whereas I may have been aware of the baby boy in her aura, this new spirit, the little girl, and her mother were fully aware of her presence. They knew something I didn't.

Tessa's pregnancy moved forward through the hot Manhattan summer. We were all anxious for the new baby to arrive. I still thought it was a boy and I was puzzled that Tessa still believed she was having a girl. We knew it wasn't twins. And then a strange thing happened one afternoon while I was out shopping for a baby gift for someone else's baby shower. I got the most vibrant mental jolt. It was so strong it felt like a physical shove, then a sudden flash followed from somewhere—like a giant cue card—that this baby Tessa was carrying was indeed a girl.

I didn't question it. I was surprised, but I knew the flash was right.

Alexandra was born in late summer, the end of August to be exact, with that very fair red-head skin, and wisps of auburn hair.

When she was four or five, I could tell without taking a second glance that this was the child in the dreams with Laura Lee that I'd dreamed about all those years before she was born. But what was the connection between them?

~

And what happened to the little boy? Did this vibrant, mischievous, auburn-haired pixie girl bounce in one day while he was snoozing and tell him she just couldn't wait, she was coming in NOW! And did she move him out?

What I'm sure of is this; while I was watching a sleepy little boy baby, Tessa and Luke's daughter was already communicating strongly with her mother. Letting her know she was on her way.

The question was, why had she appeared in those dreams of my old friend Laura Lee Brown?

Well, as these things happen, it wasn't long before Tessa and I discovered that Laura Lee had been a close friend of two of Tessa's great aunts. Do you still believe in co-incidence? They had been lifelong friends. And that explained the connection. to Laura Lee who was also my close friend. But what was *her* tie to the dream child?

There's still a lot to untangle here, but I've often wondered if at some time in a past life, Laura Lee had a baby girl of her own. I have no idea. Could it be that this same baby girl is now Luke and Tessa's daughter? Many years later, did everything come together when the timing was right, for this child to be born to Tessa?

My old friend's been gone a long time now, and all I know is that this little girl is a favorite of all of us who know her and she's exactly where she is supposed to be.

I've always been in awe of how the universe works; how everything just falls into place with the right people, at the right time.

As for the curly-haired baby boy that got bumped? He arrived as large as life and full of beams, four years later. His name is Charlie.

But before he was even *thought* of, Tessa saw him in a dream as a toddler running around at a family gathering. That would have been about two years before he was born.

~

You can't make this stuff up, lovely people. I'm not nearly that clever. And not everyone's a liar, or is suffering from some mental derangement or a bang on the head. Something else is going on. And I feel that we're only seeing the tip of the iceberg.

Chapter 12: Just Thinking . . .

Of people & things ~ of ancient places, semi-spirits and other realms.

. . . of miscarriage for one thing. It seems to me, from everything I've learned, that it's possible for a spirit to make the decision to be born at a certain time, to certain parents in a certain place. So isn't it also possible that for some reason, a spirit might change its mind and leave the embryo or fetus prematurely, causing an 'aborted' pregnancy?

So, if you've ever suffered a miscarriage, consider the possibility that perhaps none of this was your doing. It could have been that the in-coming spirit took a look around and decided it just wasn't the right time to incarnate. It just wasn't ready. Or perhaps the parents it had chosen weren't ready, so it made a sharp about turn and ended the pregnancy. So, if that has happened to you, don't despair. Very often, when the time is right for everyone, that same spirit will turn around and come back in.

Even in the case of an intentional abortion, I believe it is quite likely that for whatever reason, unbeknownst to us, this was a soul decision between the mother's spirit and the new baby's spirit, and it probably happened long before either of them was born.

Why, we wonder, would any spirit choose to go through an abortion, you ask. Why would any spirit go to the trouble and stress of preparing itself for a life on earth, choosing the circumstances to be born into, choosing its parents and siblings, and then leave?

Is it possible that both the in-coming spirit and the mother choose to abort the pregnancy–together? Had they agreed to go through a partial pregnancy and then end it abruptly simply to shed light on the problems of abortion for both mother and embryo? Or was the intention to teach us something about the continuing evolution of the soul? Maybe it was to arouse awareness of the plight of a girl or woman who was raped, or was in an incestuous and/or abusive relationship. Or was it a young girl and boy who had simply made a mistake? Perhaps it was the intention of those all of those spirits to arouse compassion instead of judgment in the rest of us.

Or was it the spirit of a badly deformed fetus with the highest intentions, who decided that by giving up its body, it could further the knowledge of fetal abnormalities?

We don't know. We can speculate as we will, but in no way am I qualified to judge the act of intentional abortion. That domain, I believe, belongs to God and the mother; a human mother who should never have been presumed to be infallible in the first place—a mother who was perhaps dealing with circumstances the rest of us know nothing about.

The spirits involved know why an abortion occurs, the Universe knows, and God knows. And all three of those entities speak from an ocean of knowledge and compassion for human frailty. If we can't do that, consider for a moment that *compassion* may be one of the things we are here to learn as we strive for perfection.

~

Then there's the topic of Pre-existence. Have we lived before? Has our eternal spirit been through many previous lives? And is it possible that whereas we may have lived on this planet, is it just as likely that we lived on other worlds in other galaxies, in other Universes? Or even in other dimensions? There may even be some of us who are experiencing our first visit away from our eternal home, some call, "Heaven". They must be living in shock. No wonder there are those that choose never to leave.

Are we, those of us who struggle with the immense challenges of earth, brave souls? Or just plain crazy? Makes you wonder.

~

There are stories—some would label them 'myths'—of the ancient worlds of Lemuria and Atlantis, where nearly three million years ago, it is said that truly human-like beings were on our planet; beings who lived long before brain structures began changing and evolving, differentiating humans from animals. They were light beings, we believe, who lived long before all of the acknowledged ages of mankind, they lived here at the very start of our evolution.

We read that some of these individuals were neither animal nor human. The legends speak of the first Atlanteans as 'not quite physical beings'. It seems that they were much more cerebral than we are today. They were emergent physical beings, but mostly mind and thought entities, with solid bodies that were just beginning to take on physical characteristics.

It sounds to me as though there was some confusion going on at the time, which may explain the odd combination of creatures from Greek, Egyptian and Roman mythology who were half animal and half human with some of the unfortunates sporting a variety of heads. I'm trying to imagine the conversation that took place in the local 'body shop', when something didn't go as planned and some hapless soul found himself with a botched project on his hands.

"Whoops! Could be wrong, but I think you handed me the wrong format, Bodikinacea! This one's got a human head and some kinda zebra-looking apparatus on the back end–what d'ya you think Cosmolikis?"

"Yup! You've got a mess there for sure. HEY! (loud whistle) Pay attention! For the last time! No stripes on the Humanicas Bodicas model! How many times do I have to tell you! Jeese! Let's move this thing along! Pick up the pace, down there!"

The Lemurians, from the lost land of Lemuria, which has been placed by some as being somewhere in the South Pacific, pre-dated the Atlanteans, and they, we're told, were not physical at all but they are instead, phantom-like beings, ghostly and ephemeral. In Roman mythology, the *lemures* means spirit.

So, isn't it interesting and full of wonder, to think that as far back as the beginnings of our earth, we might have been there? A little unusual looking perhaps, but We Were There! We could have been among the Spirits who came to the planet to test it out; perhaps, to see what kind of physiology would be needed for humans to survive in the developing, harsh conditions of the early earth? We may have been coming to earth for millions of years.

I understand too, the theory of the Big Bang, which may have given birth to our fledgling world; and the theory of Creation. Do you believe that nothing is impossible in the world of spirit? And if you believe in a creator, a God, an almighty spirit who made us all, that too fits. What fun He must have had with that Big bang. What a firework show!

The sparks flew, ashes rained and giant rocks exploded all over our corner of the Universe. What a spectacle it must have been if you were watching our planet's birth from another dimension. I like to believe we were. And I hope we there when finally clouds formed and it began to rain. Rivers ran rampant, hissing over molten lava, sending clouds of steam aloft, making more clouds that rained, and gave the earth its first oceans. Can't you just see them, spilling into the rifts and craters of the new planet and cooling the barren landscape?

Who knows how much time elapsed before the first seeds of life appeared—and how much time after that did it take a handful of spirits to get together in our eternal home and say to one another, "Let's go down and have a look!" Voila. The first explorers arrived and perhaps 'they' were us.

I believe, from many interviews with the children, and my own readings of adults, not to mention all that has been written by people like Edgar Cayce and Ian Stephenson, that we have been coming and going for a long, long time.

Chapter 13: Julie Ann

Crying inconsolably, the child pressed her face against the window. "I don't want to get off the plane! I can't leave the babies" She pointed to the air outside the window.

It was midday on a warm and sunny September day in Johnson City, Tennessee and the pre-school was letting out. A line of cars wound their way around the corner and up the driveway to the designated pick-up place where two teachers were bundling young children and their belongings into waiting vehicles.

The crowd of disheveled children was boisterous and happy that school was let out for the day, laughing and chattering, playing catch around the 'holding area'.

"Joseph Anthony!" One of the teachers shouted. "Put that stick down and stop chasing Kimmy!" She turned to her co-worker. "Please watch for Julie Ann's mom, I really would like to speak to her about something."

"I think I see her car now–just coming around the bend." She pointed to the street.

109

"Tony James!" The first young teacher lunged for the stick in the little boy's hand. "That child is going to send me slap round the bend if he doesn't start listening! Hi Mrs. Jones!" She put her head through the rolled down window of a car that had pulled to a stop in front of her. "I need to talk to you about something and I was hoping you could stop in for a few minutes tomorrow before school."

"Hi Momma!" Julie Ann piled through the back door and grabbed for a big, floppy retriever that was taking up most of the back seat.

"Sure," her mother said. "Is everything okay?" She raised her hand to shield her eyes from the sun.

"Everything's fine—nothing wrong, nothing at all. I just need to talk to you about something that's come up."

"Okay, I'll see you then. Move away from the door, Julie Ann, I want to close it." The door rolled forwards, and clicked shut, then, "Bye," she waved and drove slowly into the line of traffic wondering what her daughter's teacher wanted to talk about. Why is it, she thought, that a summons from a teacher always makes my stomach curl into a knot? Just the way it did when I was six, for Heaven's sake! Oh well, she'd find out in the morning.

~

Marilyn Jones, Julie Ann's mother arrived early the next day, before the rowdy mass of children came crashing through the gates to begin their day, and handed her little girl to the receiving teacher.

The courtyard outside the pre-school building was bathed in early morning sunlight, and the playground and classrooms were as quiet as they would ever be. The young woman walked across the courtyard and knocked on the Kindergarten door. Julie Ann's teacher opened the door with a big smile. Too big, Marilyn thought, as she was ushered through the door and into the small administrative office.

Miss Levitt, only in her first year of teaching, hesitated a moment, twirling a pencil between her fingers, and then said, "Mrs. Jones, thanks for coming," She closed the door and motioned to a chair. "Please, have a seat," she said, seating herself in a chair beside the desk. "I thought we could meet in here rather than the classroom where we might be interrupted," she cleared her throat as Julie Ann's mother sat down and folded her hands on her lap. "First, let me say how sorry I was to hear of the loss of two of your children." She watched for a reaction as Julie Ann's mother, keeping her eyes lowered, carefully set her purse down on the desk. "I . . . can't imagine what you've been through," she said. "Julie Ann told me about them and–"

Marilyn raised one of her hands to stop the young woman, and leaned forward placing her arms on the desk, lacing her fingers together. Then she looked Julie's Ann's teacher in the eye and said "Thank you. I did lose two children. It was a sad time–devastating, in fact. I miscarried twins. But it was nearly 7 years before Julie Ann was born. A long time ago."

"Oh!" The teacher looked stunned. "To hear Julie Ann talk I thought it had happened recently–it sounded as though they were babies she knows. A girl and a boy? I don't know what to say . . ."

"It's alright–really. It's not something we ever talk about but . . . I don't know why Julie Ann would bring it up,." she gave a little smile, "well, you know how kids are."

"I do indeed." The teacher relaxed, but not before noticing that the little girl's mother had been shaken by the revelation. "You should just hear some of stories I hear– well, never mind that, I just wanted to be sure that I know what to say and how you'd like me to handle the situation when it comes up again. How to respond to Julie Ann without upsetting her . . . I'm so sorry." The young woman, embarrassed and at a loss for words, reached across the desk and put her hand on the mother's arm. "We just didn't want to make things worse by being tactless."

"It's okay." Marilyn Jones replied. "I appreciate your letting me know about this." She picked up her purse. "Don't worry about it. And if she comes up with anything else, I think you should just let it be, listen to her, treat it normally and move on. I'm not sure why she's doing it, but I'll speak to her this afternoon." She shrugged. "My husband and I never discuss it, never say anything she might overhear . . . But, I guess we'll have to talk about it some." She turned to go. "I hope that helps."

"Yes. Thanks, it does. She's a sweet child."

~

What she hadn't told Miss Levitt was that a set of twins had been conceived out of wedlock, when she was just seventeen, long before she met and married Julie Ann's father. One had died in utero and the other aborted spontaneously and died within minutes of its twin.

There had never been any need to tell her husband. At least, her mother thought so, and had insisted that it would be better to say nothing. So Marilyn had kept quiet. Her mother and father were the only people who knew about the twins and how she had been sent away to have the babies. People didn't talk about such things at the time and by the time she met her husband-to-be, the whole incident was so far in the past that she hadn't even thought about telling him. Well, maybe she had, but it seemed less and less important as the years went by.

Now, her parents were no longer living, and there was no way on earth Julie Ann could have known anything about the babies.

~

The teacher closed the door behind her and leaned against the bright blue paint. It had been an awkward start to the day. She breathed deeply, blew a wisp of hair off her forehead and frowned. She had been quite sure the child knew her twin siblings. The way she talked about them— always in the present tense. The way she relayed snippets of conversation with them. . . She shook her head, looked at the clock on the wall and poured herself a cup of coffee.

~

That afternoon at pick-up time, Marilyn Jones glanced at her rearview mirror and watched the little girl snuggling up to the family dog. She was feeling uneasy by what the pre-school teacher had said that morning. What could the child possibly know about the infants she had lost? Maybe she should try to find out more from her young daughter. Try to find out where all of this was coming from, and why now.

Truth be told, this wasn't the first time the child had made reference to her brother and sister. The previous summer, when the family was flying home after a two week vacation, she and her husband noticed Julie Ann waving out of the airplane window, smiling and wiggling in her seat. They had simply looked at each other and smiled. Marilyn settled back in her seat and closed her eyes, ignoring the child until the captain's voice announced their descent and she reached over to make sure the little girl was belted in.

"What're you doing?" Julie Ann she wanted to know.

"I'm checking your seat belt. We're getting ready to land and you have to have the seat belt buckled until we get off the plane."

"No! I don't want to get off!"

"We have to. We're going to be home soon."

"Noooo! Why do I have to!"

"Come on, Julie Ann!'

The child began to cry. She clutched the window ledge and pressed her face against the window. "Noooo! I don't want to get off! I want to stay . . ." Big tears were rolling down her cheeks.

"Hush, Julie Ann! Look, you've made the window all smeary."

"I don't care!" The little girl was crying inconsolably. Her mother put her arm around her and held her. "Tell me why you don't want to get off the plane."

"I don't want to leave the babies . . . they're on the clouds!" She pointed to the air outside the aircraft. They were descending fairly fast now, and the wing was fast disappearing into a cloud bank.

"I don't see any–"

"Where'd they go!" Julie Ann wailed.

"Hush, baby. Shhush It's okay. They're no babies out there! Help me get your bag." She leaned forward to retrieve the bright green back pack under the seat in front of the little girl, who was sobbing loudly. "Here, honey, hold this," Marilyn pushed the bag towards the child who smacked it away and turned back to the window.

"What's wrong?" Her father asked.

"She says she doesn't want to get off the plane!" Nothing would quiet Julie Ann and her mother was getting worried "Look at me, Julie Ann," she cupped her hands around the child's face. "Maybe we'll see them when we land. Perhaps they'll be in the airport waiting for us." For a minute the sobs subsided, and Julie Ann took the tissue her mother offered, and wiped her nose. And then she began to cry again.

"See who?" her husband asked.

Marilyn just shrugged and shook her head. "She's okay," she had said quietly, and leaned back in her seat, closing her eyes and patting Julie Ann as the wheels clanked down and the aircraft made its final approach to the runway. She was still crying when they got off the plane with passengers and flight attendants looking on, not understanding what they were seeing.

The child finally cried herself to asleep on the drive home and nothing more was ever said about the incident.

~

She thought about that day now as they sat in the traffic line leaving school. It was long and moving slowly, and Marilyn decided to broach the subject while she had the little girl strapped in with no chance of an immediate escape. "Julie Ann, what have you been telling your teacher about two babies?" She asked.

The child hesitated. "Nothin'."

"She said you were talking about a boy and a girl baby."

"I just know those babies." She grabbed the retriever around the neck and "ruff-ruffed" in his ear.

"Will you talk to me about them one day?"

"Sure."

"You know you mustn't tell stories, don't you?"

"I'm *not!*"

"How do you know them?"

"They come and play with me."

"Where?"

118

"In my house, silly!"

"Julie—"

"They do, they do! I like David the best—he's my friend!"

Marilyn blanched and clutched the steering wheel. Her hand had accidently thumped the car horn and someone in the line honked back.

"Say that again."

"I said, I like David the best.

Marilyn's mind went back to that frightening day so many years ago when she delivered first one fetus, and then the other. The first was stillborn and the second lived for only a few minutes. She remembered the hushed voices of the nurses, of seeing the hastily wrapped bundles being hurried away. She remembered being very afraid, and when the delivery room was cleared and she was taken back to her room, she remembered the feeling of numbing loneliness that filled her.

The nurse had given her something to help her sleep, and hastily left the room. She had covered her face with a pillow and cried. She cried for herself and for the babies. She came from a rigidly religious home, and she wasn't sure whether she cried out of guilt or sorrow, she just knew she was wretchedly sad and empty. If only God would give her another chance, another baby . . . she thought. She had never felt so miserable in her life.

There was no one there to comfort her. There was no one to see her tears, so she cried some more. And cried, until finally, exhausted, she fell asleep.

She awoke to the sound of footsteps in the hallway and a soft rapping on her door before it was pushed open and a floor nurse came into the room. She pulled up a chair beside the bed, touched Marilyn's hand and spoke gently.

"How are you?" She asked.

Her eyes were red and swollen and she remembered them stinging as they had filled with tears at the first sound of kindness she had heard, and she couldn't speak.

The nurse patted her hand and said. "Did you know you were carrying twins, dear?"

She shook her head again and managed a whispered, "No."

"They were able to identify the sexes. Do you want to know what they were?"

She nodded and watched the nurse's face blurring in front of her as she told her they were a boy and a girl, and asked if she wanted to name them.

"You'll remember this for the rest of your life," she told her. "And it will be hard, but it might be easier for you later, if you give them names."

So, she named them David and Angela.

Julie Ann had no way of knowing that. The only place the names could be found was on a dusty shelf full of old and mostly forgotten medical documents, in a distant hospital's Records Department.

"How did you know their names?" She asked her daughter.

"The babies told me, silly! Mama why don't you ever talk to them?"

"I will now, my darling," Marilyn said.

"Okay!" The little girl was rapping on the window and pointing excitedly. Look Mama! There's Melanie! Can she come over? Please, please?"

And the conversation was over for now, leaving Marilyn to wonder. I will now, my darling. I'll talk to the babies.

Chapter 14: Toby

"Maaama! Mama . . ."

It's a long drive from Kansas City Mo. to Denver. Nine hours plus a few, Kevin calculated just before he and three year old Toby, left his parents home after the Thanksgiving holiday.

They had been on the road for about three hours now and he thought, not for the first time, that this midwestern state would fit in nicely with the video games from hell. There was no way out! There was no end to Kansas. Just hundreds of miles of flat nothingness and the brown mustard plains of fall that stretched endlessly towards the milky sky, blending into its cloudless void. No rim, no horizon separates land and inner space. And there's no line of demarcation–just this nebulous, surreal landscape whose only anchor to reality was the long black ribbon of asphalt under the tires of his Subaru, spinning crazily towards Denver. The Japanese engine driving the whirr of his Detroit wheels was the only sound in this hamster ball toy rolling rapidly westward.

Kevin could see how easily disorientation might set in. There was no beginning and no end to this. It was as though some weirdo mixologist–who in the hell thought that word up–had shaken this whole mustard milky crap together in his giant blender to confuse and upset the status quo. It gave the illusion of being suspended in some wild and God forsaken cocktail. He shook his head, blinking hard to ward off who knew what kind of hallucination his faked out brain might come up with at any moment. Not that he'd ever had any kind of hallucination, but if ever it was going to happen, Kansas was a likely venue for one. 'Mixologist'! What happened to 'bar tender'?

He twiddled with the knob on the car radio which only added an extra layer to the jumble of confusion that reigned inside and out. A mumbo jumbo playground of mixologist rendered music and voices, snatches of conversation fading in and out, tunes and crap he couldn't get tuned in. But at least it broke the monotony. Eventually he turned it off, opting instead for an '80's disc and drove on, riding with it through the desert on a horse with no name.

At midday they stopped in Salina, where he fed them both at a truck stop; a hamburger for him, a hot dog, no bun and a pickle for Toby and gas for the Subaru. Half an hour later they hit the road with his small son playing contentedly with a dinky truck and a floppy frog, making motor noises from the confines of his car seat. When that got old and the toddler started fussing, Kevin launched into his song repertoire belting out a sketchy version of Old McDonald that somehow got mixed up with Three Blind Mice and Hey Jude. He figured the little guy fell asleep somewhere in the middle of daa,da, da, dadada daaaa . . . so they bypassed Colby, and with the needle hitting 80, they skimmed the asphalt towards the Colorado border towns to the sounds of Bob Dylan and Eric Clapton.

The music worked for a while, but somewhere near Goodland, Kevin could feel his mind starting to drift. He ought to pull over and get some coffee, he thought for the second time in the last hour, but Toby, tightly strapped into the car seat behind him, was sound asleep and the last thing Kevin needed was an unhappy baby for the next 170 miles. He looked at the dash clock. In about half an hour Toby might be ready to eat, so he'd stop then and get something to keep them both going. He remembered a broken down desert town that should be coming up soon. It had dusty buffalo heads hanging on yellow walls inside the service station, so he bypassed a small town that was coming up on his left, and kept going.

It wasn't long before, right on cue, forty miles or so down the road, the silhouettes of a water tower and grain silos, dusty in the fading light, loomed ahead of them.

Kevin yawned widely and lowered his window to let in some fresh air. He breathed in deeply, really needing this stop. The air was damp and cold and low clouds were mounding like dirty marshmallows in the distance. A flurry of snowflakes skittered across the windshield as he pulled his head inside thinking, this is just what we need. Snow! But winter wasn't far off, so what do you expect, he thought wryly.

They drew closer, and as he slowed down to exit the freeway, he began to get a bad feeling. Why were there no cars in the parking lot? No trucks—not even a tractor on the service road—or beyond that. He pulled off Interstate 70 and cruised onto a rutted turn off that looked as though it had been abandoned by the highway department. It took him past an old motel with shutters barely clinging to its windows towards a gas station just up ahead that looked deserted. One of the tanks was twisted crookedly on its concrete base, its hose trailing in the dirt. Damn! It was shut down. Deserted. The town had shriveled up and died! There wasn't a soul anywhere that he could detect.

To make matters worse, Toby was whimpering in his sleep, so, rolling his window down again, Kevin eased back onto the interstate and hit the gas. Crap! "We're screwed, Tobes!" he said as the toddler sneezed and shifted in his chair.

126

Now, even if he wanted to stop, there was very little hope of their being any kind of a stopping place on this long, straight stretch to Denver. Starbucks was miles behind and miles ahead. There was nothing to look forward to but a cobweb of dirt roads snaking away from the freeway on either side, and asphalt trails with a dusting of snow that showed no recent tire tracks. Barbed wire fences stringed the roadside running for miles and miles to places nobody had ever heard of including McDonald's and Taco Bell. There wasn't even a cantina in sight. A burrito and a Mountain Dew wouldn't be half bad 'round about now.

It was late afternoon and the light was failing, not helped by a thick mist that drifted off the never-ending plains. The snow was coming down harder now, a half inch or more covering the brown dirt on either side of the Interstate and it was getting harder to see the road ahead. Not that that really mattered–the road ahead was exactly the same as the road behind him, dead straight and paper flat, and right now, all he wanted to do was to get home.

He searched through his snow spattered windshield for that first sight of the mountains. A person ought to be able to see those mammoths rising from the Denver plain from a hundred miles away. But you never can. You never saw them coming, never saw the jagged peaks, of the

Front Range looming thousands of feet high in front of you until they were right on top of you, only about twenty five miles away. And then all you saw was a long, low bumpy white ridge on the edge of the world. They appeared, out of nowhere as mounds of low, white cloud on the horizon. There was something very cool about that. He guessed it must have something to do with the incline of the earth as you drove up to Denver. The mountains were crouched behind the plain's mound, lying in wait, making them impossible to see until you had driven high enough and level enough to be almost nose-to-nose with them. Nose-to-nose with a Rocky Mountain. Cool.

Kevin shook his head and blinked his eyes rapidly. As tired as he was he'd better watch he didn't plough right into one of them. He'd ploughed down them more times than he cared to remember, and they were solid. Rock hard and solid.

He began praying for a roadside stop; a cantina, anything that had a pot of coffee or a soda machine. Visibility was getting worse as evening fell and dense swaths of mist rolled by on either side of the car, drifting towards him like thick cotton blowing across the plain. Toby whimpered from the back seat, but didn't stir. Kevin glanced at his rear-view mirror and saw the little boy's head lolling to one side, his eyes tight shut. He envied him.

128

He made himself think of things that would engage his mind and keep him alert. Annie from two houses down the street would be at his house right about now feeding Dinner Wap. That was what Toby called the cat whose given name was actually Ginger Snap. A large furry, orange mutt of a cat that followed Toby around 'chattering' at him like a mother hen, waiting for crumbs to fall.

He smiled at the thought. 'Dinner Wap' liked Annie a lot. So did Toby. A senior in high school now, she took care of him whenever Kevin could get her to baby sit. They all liked Annie.

The wind had begun to blow now and a mix of new snow and fog swept across the hood of the Subaru. He scrunched over the steering wheel focusing his eyes on the road, squinting around the wipers. Toby started to cry and Kevin groaned. Not now, little guy! He turned his fog lights on and lowered his high beams. Toby let out a serious howl and he could hear him revving up for a major crying jag.

"Hey, Toby! It's okay, don't cry man . . . not far now. We'll be home soon."

"Whaaa . . ." the crying got louder and more insistent as Kevin reached behind him to pat the baby's

leg. "Hey, big fella! Gonna see Annie soon!" And that only made him holler louder.

"Noooooo!" It wasn't long before the crying began to get frantic.

Jeese! "The wheels on the bus go 'round an' . . . help me out, buddy."

"Nooooooo! Noooo!" The baby sobbed.

"Okay no wheels, screw the wheels, dude! Here we go." Kevin pounded the steering wheel and belted out "From the halls of Montezu-uma to the shores of Tripoli . . . Sing, Tobes!"

For what may have been a microsecond, he turned his head to smile at his son, and that was when he first saw the row of lights, on the back of a Mac truck, looming straight in front of him. The Subaru was within inches of the trucker's rear bumper. Instinct took over and Kevin swerved to avoid it as he watched the huge vehicle spin out on the icy road, topple and skate along the slippery highway on its side.

The last thing he saw was one of the giant rear wheels fly off the vehicle and hit the side of his car.

~

The next thing he became aware of was the inside of an ambulance. White and metallic and smelling of antiseptics. He heard himself asking for Toby. He could taste blood in his mouth and was aware that he could barely form the words. His neck was braced and his jaw was secured in some sort of a bridle, by the feel of it.

"Toby . . ." He tried again.

"He's asking for the baby," a state trooper shouted to one of the paramedics alongside the road.

"Tell him we sent him on ahead."

"He's on his way to Denver, buddy." the trooper told Kevin. "The baby's already on his way to Denver."

"He's alive–you're both alive." The EMT, who had come up to the back door, put his hand on Kevin's shoulder. "Truck driver's not so lucky," he said. "And you're pretty banged up. Just don't try to talk, man, they'll have that jaw fixed right quick–soon's we can get you to the city." He turned to leave.

And that was the last thing Kevin heard before he woke up in Denver's big Trauma Center in a brightly lit room with people in green scrubs moving all around him. And then everything went black again.

~

Early the next morning, Kevin came to in a hospital room with an intern standing at the foot of his bed scribbling on a chart. "Whersh's Toby?" he asked

"Hi there! You're doing pretty well after tangling with a dump truck!" The young intern smiled at him and handed the chart to a nearby nurse. "Your son is holding his own right now, and we're hoping for a lot of improvement today." He walked around to the side of his bed.

"Whas tha' mean?" Damn, they had his mouth full of something obnoxious and soggy.

"He's alive. That's the good news." He bent down and shone a light into Kevin's eyes. "We're helping him breathe right now, but we hope that'll change today and he'll start breathing on his own."

Kevin started to lift himself up and a gentle hand pushed him back down against the pillows. "Lie still," a nurse said.

"Where ish he? Damn! Can't shpeak!"

The intern seated himself on the edge of the bed. "The inside of your mouth is swollen from the surgery we did on your jaw last night. That should go down before long. We've also got a bale of cotton tucked in there to keep you from talking so much." The young doctor smiled broadly.

Real joker, this one, Kevin thought grumpily

"Try not to speak. Keep those bones as still as possible– let them heal." He asked the nurse to hand him another chart.

"Your son, Toby is in the Pediatric ICU in serious condition." He told Kevin. "Looks like he was unconscious when they brought him in last evening and has still not regained consciousness."

"He's–?" Kevin was having difficulty processing the doctor's words.

"He's in a coma. But as I said, we're hoping that will change today. His pediatrician will be in soon and he'll be able to give you a better understanding than I can. As well as the latest update. In the meantime," he continued, "we have called your family and your mom and dad are on their way here."

"Oh God–Wha' 'appened?" Kevin tried to raise his arm to cover his eyes but it was attached to an IV. that wouldn't let him.

"The police report I read said that a truck in front of you lost control and one of its wheels flew off almost demolishing the side of the car where you son was seated."

"Jesus!" He could feel tears burning behind his eyelids. "Wanna shee him."

"I'll get someone to help you. You have a broken shoulder and a concussion. Bruise the size of Texas where your seatbelt kept you from flying through the windshield, and three broken ribs. And the lower jaw is broken. You're banged up, like I said, and you're going to feel it when you start to move."

~

His parents flew in from Kansas City. Friends and family members came and went as they began a vigil praying for the baby to wake up. The hours ticked by with excruciating slowness. Days turned into nights that turned into new days, and hope began to fade.

Kevin was released from hospital on the sixth day, and still the child lay unconscious. He was the only baby in the unit so a cot was moved into the room so his father could stay with him at night.

On the eleventh day they received a call from the hospital. It was the call they had all been praying and hoping for. Toby was showing signs of improvement.

Within an hour, his family was at his bedside watching the little boy, still not quite there, move his hand, his fingers–and then a leg.

"He's coming out of it," his nurse said. She and an aide were standing beside the bed, working on the breathing tube. "He started breathing on his own a few hours ago," she told them. "We just left it in to make sure he was going to be okay. There! We got it, big fella." She carefully lifted the concertinaed plastic tube from Toby's mouth and handed it to the aid. "C'mon, let's see you breathe, Toby." She watched as the baby's chest rose.

Kevin saw it move too.

"That's it!" the child's nurse said quietly. "Breath now. There you go! That's the way." She smiled as he took his first completely unassisted lungful of air and let it out. And then another.

Unaware that he had been holding his breath, Kevin felt himself exhale as his son's breathing settled into an even rhythm. There was a collective sigh in the room and suddenly everyone was crying and smiling, laughing and hugging each other.

Then Toby opened his eyes.

"Look!" someone said.

The baby stared unseeingly at all the people around his bed who had turned around to see. "He's opening his eyes," his grandmother whispered. Nobody moved. "What's he doing?" She asked the nurse. "He's looking right past us!"

His eyes were scanning the room, looking over and beyond them. It was almost as though he didn't recognize anyone. He seemed to be searching for something, or someone, that no one else could see.

"Hey, Toby—you woke up, little buddy!" Kevin's eyes filled with tears as he started to reach for his son who slowly opened his mouth and began to cry.

"Mama!" The toddler's eyes seemed to be looking straight through his father. "*Mamaaa!*" His arms reached out, his hands opened and closed in the way a young child will do when he or she wants to be picked up. "Where Mama?" he cried. He screwed his eyes shut and rubbed his fist over his mouth. "Maama! Where'd Mama go?" Nobody said a word. "*Maama!*"

Kevin leaned towards him and cupped his hands under the child's body. "Daddy's here, boy. Don't cry. Daddy's got ya!" Toby was gulping air and crying hard, pushing his father away. The nurse, who had been standing back, took a step forward.

The toddler's arms were stretched out, still reaching for someone beyond Kevin, his little fists opening and shutting as though trying to grasp something no one else could see. "*I wan' Mama!* Where's Mama? *Where'd Mama go?*"

Kevin held the baby as tightly as he could, his injured ribs screaming with the effort. "You're alright now, son. Daddy's here. Shhh, don't cry, Toby. You're okay now." His own tears mingled with Toby's, and slowly, the boy's crying subsided to a soft whine. His grandmother put her hand on the baby's back. Her eyes too were filled with tears as she looked around for a tissue. The room was silent. Nobody spoke.

The nurse's aide looked from one to the other of them. "Where is his mother?" She asked.

"Toby's mother died in childbirth," Kevin's father told her. "He never knew her. He's never even seen a picture of her."

Kevin had removed all the pictures of his young wife not long after Toby was born, his own grief too hard to bear with reminders of her everywhere he looked. There would be time enough to show them to Toby, he'd reasoned. But that time hadn't come yet.

"I don't understand . . ." the aide looked perplexed.

"Hmmph! Well, you're not the only one!" Kevin's father said. "But there's no doubt in my mind, he thinks she's here!"

~

That'll make you scratch your head and call in the Marines! Medical science doesn't know the answer. Only Toby does. Is it possible that his mother was with him while he lay in a coma for day after day?

There is still so much we don't know about the consciousness known as 'coma'. We read snatches of information about post-coma memories of dreams, nightmares, and such. There's also some evidence that a comatose person is able to hear you when you speak. There's so little to go on. I'd like to see just one headline that proclaims there's been a massive breakthrough in neuroscience that allows us to know what really goes on while someone is supposedly out of reach, locked deep in the realms of the currently unknown.

What I believe is this: The human brain is a part of our physiology. Of course you knew that. It is an organ like all the other organs. Ditto. There is nothing mystical about it, except that we don't know much about it. When it is physically impaired or severely injured, it is as sick and non-functional as any other part of the human body; as sick as a mangled arm or leg. The difference with the brain is that when it crashes traumatically, so does everything else. It's like The Mother Board.

There's a lot of physical unraveling to do before we gain the knowledge necessary to fully understand it.

Here's why I think that neuro-science is having such a difficult time sorting through the different levels of consciousness as we understand them now: Could it be that it's because there is a separate consciousness, a non-physical consciousness that works within us, completely independently of the human brain? We're seeing more and more evidence of that all the time, but because it's mostly from personal experience and accounts, it doesn't carry much weight with the folks whose job it is to discern fact from fiction.

The way I see it, is that as long as we continue to mistrust and dismiss the realms of metaphysics and its inter-connectivity with the physical, the longer it will take to sort it all out.

The fact of the matter is that it is becoming increasingly negligent and difficult to ignore the possibility of a separate entity or intelligence that's connected to every human being. Many would call it, "the spirit" or the soul. It's a separate intelligence or entity that maintains every one of its faculties even after traumatic brain injury.

I believe it is the soul that incarnated with you, who came to earth to learn from your human experience. And I can't imagine what it's thinking when it suddenly realizes that the engine that drives its humanity is, in many cases, after severe injury, Finished.

There are multiple reports from near death experiencers, multiple books written, and plenty of documentaries produced that tell us that the soul will stay around in a hospital room watching the medical proceedings, or wander off, visiting friends or relatives to try and give them a heads-up of what's going on with its person. You've heard the stories. "Out of the blue, I got this compelling feeling that there was something wrong with my sister." There are also many such stories about people who have passed on. A mother, father or close friend will find a way to let loved ones know what's happened; sometimes after the fact of his or her demise, sometimes before. That is NOT the human brain calling, my friends.

Plainly, there are too many accounts from too many different sources for the whole thing to be 'co-incidence'.

So, with that in mind, it makes sense to me to think that Toby's soul was probably with his mother's after the car accident, and for all the days he was unreachable to everyone else.

I can only imagine what he will do when he sees her picture for the first time.

Chapter 15: Liza

"Why're all those people cryin,' Mama?"

Liza was five years old when she was taken to her grandmother's funeral.

"We're going to see my Gramma at the funnel home and that they're letting me wear my best Sunday dress. It's dark blue satin, like the night time looks when I stay at Gramma's farm. And it's got this white lacy collar that Mama calls 'croshay', or something or 'nother, and black shiny shoes.

I just know I always feel pretty in that dress. It makes me feel like Cinderella but when I started to twirl and shout "Yay! We're going to see Gramma!" and clapped my hands at the Funnel place, Mama said, "Stop it, Liza!"

She's been acting kind'a mad and sad all at the same time. I don't understand. I know she's sad because I saw her crying today, and yesterday. She says something's happened to Gramma, but I don't know what! I heard Miss Gladys tell her that they used to call it galloping newmanya or something. So I figure it's a horse got loose or something. Grandpa used to have a horse.

I think Mama's confused too. She says everything's moving so fast, she can't think. That must be some horse! Then when I hum and twirl again, quietly this time, she yells in this really mad voice, "Stop it Liza! Stop behaving like that! It's wrong! You've just lost your grandmother! You shouldn't be acting up this way!"

What I what to know is how did I lose my grandmother? I didn't lose Gramma! She was in my room last night. So I ask, "When did Gramma get lost, Mama?"

"Oh, Liza!" She puts both her hands on the side of her face like she does when she doesn't know what to say, then she smoothes my hair back and says, "It's just not okay to be clapping and smiling like that with Gramma being dead only four days."

"But you said we're going to see Gramma . . ."

Then she kneels down in front of me like she does when she has something really, really important to say and she says, "Gramma is dead, Liza. We're going to say goodbye to her."

I can tell she's trying not to cry so I decide not to ask her why we're going to say goodbye when we haven't even

143

said 'hello' to her today. So I just say, "Okay," in a little voice. "Can we go now?"

She nods and goes back inside and I whirl away in my shiny shoes and run outside clapping my hands and singing, "We gonna see Gramma! We gonna see Gramma!" Then I see Samson come runnin' from the side of the house. He's my dog.

"Hi, puppy!" When I bend over and clap hands on my knees he comes running so fast, I'm thinking he might trip and roll over like he does when he gets going too quickly. That happens to me sometimes too.

"Come here, Sammy," I call and put my arms around his neck feeling his floppy ears tickle my nose making me laugh. "I'll ask Mama if you can go too."

But when I ask, they say, "No!" like I asked to take him to church or something! They don't let him go there neither. I guess the God person doesn't have a dog. If he did he'd let Sammy come visit. I guess no one wants Sammy at the funnel place either.

But that's okay. I'm excited about going to see Gramma! So I just wave when my daddy puts him in his cage. "See you soon, Sammy!"

There are big, tall trees at the funnel home and we have to park a long way away. I've never seen so many cars all together in one place. Ouch! My shoe's pinching. "Is this the funnel place, Mama?" I ask as she takes my hand and my brother's and we walk across the parking lot. She doesn't answer me an' my shoe's still pinching but its prob'ly not a good time to tell her that either.

The air inside makes my nose itch and suddenly this giant sneeze flies out of me. It's hot too, an' full of flowers. Everywhere I look there are more an' more flowers! I never saw so many flowers in my life. An' mama says there's going to cake and stuff too. Yay, maybe it's like a party or something. I look for Gramma but I don't see her—just alla these people walkin' 'round and lookin' at flowers and things. Maybe the flowers are making them sneeze too because a whole bunch of them are mopping their eyes and noses. They got lots of roses and flowers standing around this long silvery looking box they're all lookin' at. I want to ask Mama why someone brought that box in here but my dad's hugging her and all these people keep coming up to talk to us.

Mrs. Boone from the dress shop in town, where they got my blue satin dress, gives my brother a kiss and I giggle as I watch him wiping it off his cheek with a mean look. He's not s'posed to do that. You're s'posed to be happy when someone likes you enough to kiss you, Mama says. But I don't blame him. I hope Mrs. Boone doesn't like me enough to kiss me, but just in case, I'm hiding behind daddy's legs so she can't see me.

"I don't see Gramma," I tell my brother, standing on tiptoe and trying to see over the people. "Why'd Mrs. Jenks put her flowers on that box?" I point at one of the friends who's moving away from the box leaving her flowers on the closed lid. "Mama, Mrs. Jenks forgot her flowers," I squeeze my mother's hand.

"She's left them for Gramma," she says. "She's sending Gramma off with some roses," Mama slipped her arm around my shoulders and sniffed.

That didn't make a bit of sense to me. "Why, Mama? Gramma's got her own flowers at the farm!" I said and watched Mama close her eyes and take a deep breath.

"It's just what people do when someone is going away."

"But Gramma didn't go away," I say, but I don't think she hears me 'cos two more friends stop to talk to her. I look back at the big box. There's a line of people walking past it now. About a hun'red if you ask me. Some of them stop for a moment, and then keep going. I want to know what's inside the box, and why they're all actin' sad.

"Why're they cryin', Mama?" I tug her skirt. This isn't a good party.

"'Coz they're *saying goodbye to Gramma*, silly!" Kenny my brother said.

"Why are they going to that box?"

"Because Gramma's inside it, that's why."

"No! She's not!" How could he tell such a lie! "Mama, he just tol' me a fib! He said . . ."

"Hush, Liza!" My daddy said.

"But . . . OW!" He squeezed my arm and' did this loud whisper in my ear.

"I don't want to hear anymore. You hear me? Keep quite."

This party was NOT fun! I want to go home but just as I think that, Gramma waves to me. There she is! I knew she wasn't in that box! She looks so pretty . . . her hair's a gold color–It used to be gray! I smile at her and tug at my daddy's hand. I want him to let go of me so I can run to her.

"Liza! Be still!"

"But I want to see Gramma! Let me go!"

"You can't see Gramma, we told you she's not here—"

"Yes, she is! Kenny says she's in that box! But she's not inside that box! She's over there!" I pull my arm away from him real hard point to the corner of the room behind the silver box and begin to cry. "I want to go to Gramma!" I cry. "Why can't I go?"

He turns away from me to talk to Jack the fence fixer man and I see Gramma by the flowers again. She's smiling at me and saying, 'Don't cry, Liza.' I gulp and smile and call softly to her, not taking my eyes off her in case she moves away again. "Hi, Gramma!"

"Now who's tellin' lies?" My brother says. "Mama, Liza's telling lies . . ."

"Liza?" That was my Mama.

"No, I'm not! He said Gramma's in that box an' she's not, she's over there." Once again, I point to the corner of the room, trying to make them look. Why couldn't they see her? She was all shiny like light, "Can't you see her?"

"You are too telling lies!" Kenny turned to his mother. "She said Gramma's over there behind the flowers–in that corner!"

"'Cos she is!" I said stubbornly. "I can see her. Mama can you see her?" I'm staring at mama, really wanting her to tell me she sees Gramma. "Can you see Gramma?"

"Hush, Liza. No, I cannot see her. Your brother's right, she's inside that box that's called a casket." She looks at my dad and shakes her head, and he says we're being bad. Why don't they believe me?

"Stop telling me she's in that box when she's not!" I cry. "I can see her! Look over there–an' there's people with her–shiny people. Look Mama, look!" People are looking at me with cross faces. My Mama looks like she's going to cry again, and then Millie, she's my cousin, comes over and kneels down beside me and asks me if I want to go outside with her. I nod.

My mother tries to smile at Millie and says "Thank you!" and begins to cry again watching as we walk towards the door of the Funnel Home. I like Millie, so I just wave and tell Gramma I'll see her later.

~

That night when Mama puts me to bed she hugs me very closely and I can tell she's still sad. "I'm glad you saw Gramma," she whispered. "I miss her a lot."

"Don't cry, Mama, she'll be back." I whispered to her and put my hand up and touched her cheek. "Gramma's real pretty now! She says she likes her new blue dress."

I watch Mama's eyes grow real big. I hope they won't pop out of her face like that little dog we saw at the park one day. They said he was a terror dog who lives in Boston. I don't know where Boston is but his eyes sure were funny. I giggled.

"What did you say, Liza?"

"I said Gramma likes her new—"

"That's what I thought you said. I can't believe my ears!"

So I tell her again that Gramma likes the blue dress. "I wanted to tell you that in the funnel place!"

"Yes–you did," she says, but I can see she's thinkin' 'bout something else.

Then she holds my arms and looks at me funny, and says, "But. . .but how did you know about the blue dress? You've never seen it! I bought it for Gramma on my last trip to the city and I put it away! What else did she say?"

"She says, 'don't you cry!'

And then Mama smiles at me for the first time that day. "I don't understand any of this," she says softly. "But I do know you're not imagining that you saw Gramma in her new blue dress today– a dress you never saw."

Who knows what 'maginin' means. All I know is I saw the blue dress on Gramma today when she was standin' by the flowers. Didn't everybody? An' she was smilin' an' happy, so I still don't know why all those people were crying. It must'a bin the flowers.

~

Perhaps a funeral isn't the place for heart-to-hearts when a child belts out "NO, Gramma's NOT in the box! I can see her over there by the flowers!"

You could say, "Do you mean those white lilies?" This might calm her down and at least, this way, her unsettling announcement that Gramma's out of the box isn't shuffled under the rug. But most people aren't thinking that clearly at a mother's funeral and who can blame them.

Perhaps one day that mother's curiosity gets the better of her she brings up the subject with Liza again. There's so much she could learn Because wouldn't this be the perfect little channel for Gramma to let them know she was fine? To speak to them through the answers of a young child who is very sure of what's she's seen? How comforting it would be to know that dying was not the end of her life, to know that she still lives. Young and pretty again, and still in their lives.

Chapter 16: People Who Wonder

. . . sometimes it does take a paradigm shift in perception to believe what they're hearing.

If a parent is curious about finding out, and getting to the root of stories about things that seem too fantastic to believe, stories of people and things others are unable to see, this is the way to do it. Just ask. It's been my experience that children enjoy sharing these experiences. They like the attention and are happy when someone is interested enough to want to hear about it, and will gladly bend your ear for as long as you can stand it.

It's also true that most people in our Western culture are uncomfortable talking about death. To anyone. Let, alone a child. And sometimes, parents are just too busy to take the time.

Others fear the worst. What if, God forbid, their child has said something about visiting with cousin Nellie (long deceased) down by the river?

For sure, the child must be psychologically messed up. "I've never heard such nonsense!" Another aunt might declare. "Obviously it comes from the father's side of the family! Wasn't there a batty old aunt somewhere in Texas? The one they had to keep in her room so she wouldn't disturb the household?"

And that really gets Mom going. "We'd better find a therapist! What if she was brain damaged at birth . . . oh no! Quick! Call someone!

It's no wonder people panic. With all the parenting 'How To' books crowding bookshelves in every home, not one of them asks the question "What if she really did see something?"

You won't find any such thing in traditional books on child-rearing, so taking that thought a little further, a parent could take it upon himself, or herself, to think "What if I asked my child that question?" Why go to a therapist or his book, who didn't think this perception was important enough to write about in the first place? That child right in front of you has the answers.

Of course, in many cases it's much easier to believe a therapist who says, "No such thing!" That's the way most of us have been conditioned to think, and it really does require a paradigm shift in perception to attempt to believe anything else. But it's worth the try. It's a great opportunity to ask the child all the questions you can think of. You'll get answers. And, as fantastic as it sounds, you're probably getting the whole truth.

That's the time to go looking for other people who've had some of the same experiences. Listen to their stories. This is when you might get the urge to read books like this one, written by people who've experienced what you're just beginning to wonder about; to attend workshops on spirituality or join a study group. They're all sources of information, good bad or in-between. Like all sources of any information. One thing you'll notice is that there are multiple similarities in all the thousands of accounts and discussions. Millions of people over thousands of millennia can't all be bonkers or just plain delusional.

So many people, not through any fault of their own, are saddled with religions that persist in teaching that all discussion of Spirit sightings, communication etc. is straight from Hell. And occasionally I get this question that comes from someone who comes from an intensely religious background, "Where can I find some literature on what you're saying? I need something that will back up the subject matter of your books."

155

When I say, "Start with The Holy Bible" the shocked look on their faces is quite impressive. I say that because the Christian Bible, in my opinion, is the very finest resource communication, faith healings and angels. And in the New Testament, it starts with Jesus Christ.

~

I've found that the best approach to all this is not to let it confuse you. Focus on the subjects that interest you, take what you can use, and leave the rest. Enlist your intuition and draw your own conclusions.

The great thing about this sort of exploration is that when you make the effort to understand your child's "whimsies" you're opening your own awareness and taking a quantum leap into a world of never-ending exploration. You're pushing the frontiers of your own knowledge and the act of doing that may make all the difference in yours and other people's lives.

To my readers who are more traditionally inclined in their beliefs, I would like to add that my own beliefs do not exclude the great religions of the world. It would be impossible to do that. Rather, they expand them.

~

Do you ever wonder? The only unchangeable thing about living is that change is constant. Things are changing all around us and people are becoming much more open to the idea that there's a lot more to this life we're living than is easily apparent. Spiritualists will tell you the veil between dimensions has been thinning rapidly since the last half of the 20th century. And that's just one of the reasons so many more of us are able to 'see', hear and sense the unexplained phenomena all around us.

We're living in a new century and it's a very different world than it was forty or fifty years ago, and in this new world when we have masses of prior knowledge to build on, things can change very fast.

Thanks to the internet, there is a bottomless well full of information that people can tap into. There is also a bottomless well of misinformation, so proceed with caution. Above all, listen to your inner voice and trust your gut feelings. That's where the true knowledge lies.

Back in the '60's, when I was much younger than I am now, people were traipsing off to the ashrams and temples of India to 'find themselves'. Somewhere among the rich aromas of spices, and over-flowing gutters and animal and human waste, they hoped to find the answers they were looking for. Amid the swirl of scarlet hibiscus, saffron and gold bangles, the Western world disappeared and western minds opened up with ease to the ancient teachings of the east. When transcendence became the trendiest and most important mind-set to achieve, Buddhism became the rage as being the font of all transcendental enlightenment, and sitting cross-legged, beside an incense fire, swaying with the overload of strange sensations, transcendence came easily.

Or, more easely than it did in Woodstock or Washington DC or San Francisco where mind-altering drugs were among the trend-setters of the day that could be used in pursuit of inner peace. . Sometimes with tragic consequences.

The truths of the East are still ours to explore and to build on, but there is another truth: And it's right in our own back yard. It's the world within us all that holds everything known or unknown far beyond our natural boundaries. Awareness is the key.

There is also a much more tangible universe out there. Notice how television stations have been loading up their programming with ghost stories. Bookstores now have whole sections dedicated to 'New Age' literature. You'll find everything from Deepak Chopra and his Hindu Spiritualism to Wicca and Magick, Tarot and I Ching. There are dream manuals and books on Spirit Communication, animal and human spirits, and everything in between, including extra-terrestrial spirits and healers. And in the Fiction and Non-Fiction sections of any library of bookstore, writers cram the shelves with their stories of the hereafter. We can't get enough of them. We're explorers, after all.

Chapter 17: Of Ghosts & Goblins

"A curtain billows out from a dusty window. Coyotes howl . . .

Right beside the Travel Maps and Atlas sections in the bookstores and Visitor's Centers around the country, there are books and pamphlets full of ghostly places along just about any route you choose, or any town or city you decide to stop in for the night. It tweaks your interest, and you might think, "Let's stay in this Inn! They say it's got a ghost."

It all looks pretty normal as you drive up–except for the ivy clinging to the walls, and the broken chimney pot, leaning drunkenly to one side. Something rustles in the azaleas that line the walkway as you head for the front door, making you drop your sun glasses and take a step back. So you take a deep breath thinking, probably just a grasshopper. But then, lying there that night in the comforting warmth of the cozy inn loft, thinking to yourself that the bedroom's quite pretty. You like the way they've looped the blue and white striped curtains. But wait! Did that curtain on the dormer move? Hmm. That's funny–the window is closed so where did the breeze come from? If you're like me you'll be looking for an air vent somewhere close by. But you'll quickly discover that there's no air vent.

Still wondering about the breeze, you become aware of the clip clop of horses hooves you can hear on the road below–or maybe you can't. Can you? Coyotes are howling in the hills, and an owl hoots from a nearby cottonwood. Funny how it's becoming uncomfortably warm in this cozy inn all of a sudden, and it's time to switch the bedside light on and sit bolt upright in your bed. But just as you reach for the lamp switch, the curtain billows away from the dusty window.

That does it! You waste no time in diving under the covers for the safety of the known dark.

Unless you are a child.

If you were a child, you might sit up straight in bed and watch the curtain for a bit. And then figuring something was there, you might say, "Who's there? Why are you blowing the curtain?" If you were a child, you probably wouldn't be afraid. You might ask, "What's your name?" And the figure that materializes beside the curtain might tell you.

It would seem quite natural to you, as a child, that this person appeared out of nowhere, and is now blowing the drapes around. Nothing scary there. Perhaps you know this entity from the other side. You might even ask if he had ridden here on those horses outside. A child would find nothing strange or frightening about any of this, unless he had been frightened previously by someone else living in his circle of acquaintances.

Fear must be taught, and you can never rule out an older sibling, I suppose, whose aim it is to scare the wits out of a baby brother, probably because he himself is secretly scared of the dark, and ghostly animals and scary people. Because someone in the third grade told him to be, is my guess. Or maybe it's just too much Saturday morning TV and Scooby Doo.

Ghost tours in carriages that rattle over the cobblestones of old towns are centuries old and haven't lost any of their allure in this 21st Century. And they are no longer confined to New Orleans, Charleston, the Wild West and the battlefields of old wars. Famously 'haunted' places abound with enough gore and questionable Hollywood imagination to sink a battleship. Country inns attract people with stories of resident ghosts, and the sounds of thumping and banging coming from disincarnates skulking around in musty attics and hallways. Or the lonely cry of a long lost child in the woods. All of it is guaranteed to raise the hairs on the back of your necks and send shivers down your spine. If you happen to be pre-disposed to nerves, you might even (don't even think it!) *dampen your drawers.*

~

I like the story of one guest who stayed in a two hundred year old inn, in an old town out west, with a name that sounded like Hangman's Gulch, who swore he saw a row boat on the lake outside his window at 2:00 a.m. one morning; accompanied by the cries and wails of drowning men.

Well, his tale at breakfast the next morning, created a scurrying of guests for the door, hardly bothering to pack their bags, and churned the innkeepers into an uproar of denial.

Couldn't they see there WAS no lake? There wasn't even a water hole for a hundred miles, dagummet—which should have been a clue to the fact that there was no boat either, and no drowning men. It wasn't enough though, to stem the exodus of scared silly guests. Nor could they be persuaded, when the idea was floated, (no pun intended) that the dreamer was known to have developed a liking for the local home brew. Not to mention the company of the late night ladies of the Shoot 'em Up Saloon next door.

This might have worked, but lost traction when one of those late night, slightly transparent ladies wafted down the stairs, delicately holding her skirt off the ground to expose a shapely ankle, and made the remark that, in her opinion, it was quite possible that there were–um, phantoms afoot.

Actually, all of the stories are entertaining and fun to hear, to scoff at, or to sit there listening to in disbelief, silently wondering, 'What If–they're true?'

Some of them, I have no doubt, have some basis in truth. In many others, whereas there may be some truth, that truth may have to be dug out from under the colorful embellishments of many different story tellers, and may hundreds of years. The above story's entertainment value had probably grown enormously since the inn, a wooden box of a hotel on a dusty main street, first opened its doors as Miss Mable's Rest and Comfort House For Gentlemen and their Ladies.

It's still entertaining, and every story may tug you a little further along the route to discovery, but you don't really need any of that to start your journey down the path to other worlds. Simply by picking up a book of ghost stories, you know the seed of curiosity inside you is alive and well.

164

~

What *can* you believe? Who's being honest and who's lying through their teeth? We can't be sure. One thing we can be sure of is that every one of us has the ability within us to wonder about, discern for ourselves, any run in or awareness we've had of any 'ghostly,' experiences, and always keeping an open mind, draw our own conclusions.

Most of us have had at least one brush with a 'ghost'. You may or may not have noticed it, but think back to the time you thought you felt someone sitting on the end of your bed. But when you kicked out or leapt for the light switch, there was no one there. You probably just turned over and went back to sleep. But, I bet you thought about the 'incident' at least once the next day thinking, I know there was someone there. I felt the bed sag! Huh! Odd. But, for Pete's sake! It had to be a dream! Didn't it?

And wasn't it strange how, in another 'dream', you had the distinct impression of your Uncle Jeb, who had been dead for years, sitting on the rocker on the porch, looking more real and younger and more peaceful than you've ever seen him? You know very well he's dead and that this is just a dream, because you were a pall bearer at his funeral. Yet you also KNOW that's him sitting in the rocker! The real, live him all fleshed out and dandy! And you don't care

165

what anyone says, you saw Jeb on the porch, doggone it!. Not dead, or half-dead–but very much alive and well! You blink, and shake your head.

Your stomach growls and you're thinking maybe you need a handful of Tums. Obviously your over-active imagination is in high gear which is most likely the result of the Indian curry you ate the night before. So, you let it go, grab for a box of crackers and shove the thought aside.

Then one day, perhaps in a week or two, a month or a year or two, something tweaks the memory of that 'dream' and you want to find out more. What was it that made you think of Uncle Jeb in the first place? You hadn't thought of him for a very long time. Could it have been a ghostly tweak on the lobe of your ear?

The way you find out more, is by placing one foot in front of the other on the misty path ahead of you. You can't see it clearly, but you know it's there. You can even see the way it's headed, even though you can't yet see the curves, the twists and turns or the destination. But that seed of curiosity is alive and squirming to break through the hard shell of doubt that still exists.

The first step along that path happens by putting aside the notion that it was a dream, coincidence or imagination, and starting to wonder instead if it was indeed, an actual visit.

You have just turned the light on that seed of exploration and enabled the fascinating process of awareness to grow. You have approached and navigated the first curve in the road.

The more you allow yourself to ponder the impossible, the more you'll become aware of things you can't explain, so you'll start to read and research and explore. Soon you will begin to build a solid base for your own tower of information that will be built on all the bricks of knowledge that you'll pick up along the way. Your powers of concentration, observation and discernment will build on each other too, and the engine of awareness will drive you forward, for it is Awareness that allows you to think, and to follow the What If? And, to wonder what's around the next corner.

It might be a good time to have a word with Uncle Jeb. (Yes, of course you were there when they buried him) You could open the conversation, with something like, "Look, I know I saw you—but you have to admit that's pretty weird and unbelievable to most people, me included. So, if I'm right, and you can hear me, would you mind giving me a sign?"

It doesn't matter what kind of sign. Ask for a sailboat. So what if it's winter. He'll find a sailboat for you. It might be a picture of one on a magazine cover that you just happen to pick up a couple of hours later. And if you just shake your head and say, "Nah!" in disbelief, he will probably cause an email from a friend to appear inviting you to go sailing around the Cape next summer! Or a lady friend may give you a bottle of Old Spice with its world famous logo, a galleon, etched on the front of the bottle. Be aware. Be especially aware when, on the ride home from work, the radio springs the "Sailing" song from its airwaves.

Something else you'll discover is that your old uncle has probably been around you for a while, just waiting for you to acknowledge him. And that's the next step along the path. Acknowledging to yourself, that this is odd—you have no explanation handy, it may need looking into.

The truth, I've found, is that they love to hear from us. And if you can open the door for them, just a crack, they'll find you, and the reunion with that much loved person will be—humor me—out of this world. You'll feel wonder and maybe a little doubt, but not for long. Most of all, you'll be greatly comforted and consoled. It's a very transformational thing.

~

If you want company on your search, listen to the children. Listen to the young people in your life. They're all part of your journey of exploration, and they know so much more than you can possibly imagine.

Chapter: 18: Fact or Fantasy?

"Ohhhh, I'm so scared of the Devil!"

You don't need me to tell you that some children have vivid imaginations. That's something to always keep in mind when researching this subject. In fact imagination and 'suggestion' are two of the first things to rule out when trying to authenticate a story you're hearing.

I don't believe that young children are lying–that's a big word–but you may wonder how much of a part their imagination is playing at any given time. And if you suspect that they're making up this weird and wonderful story, that's when you begin to delve into their young lives a little. You won't have to probe or dig too deeply for what you need. The well of information they have is shallow and clear, and I've found that you'll be able to discern fact from fiction very quickly. And in the course of this investigation you may even find that you've uncovered a future best-selling author.

A good place to start is to question them about the amount of television they've been exposed to. Getting the right answer to this question is sometimes tricky, and it's usually the adults who make it complicated. A parent may not want to admit that her child watches a lot of television, or plays video games. Come on! Everyone uses the TV as a baby sitter from time to time, don't they? Especially when you have things to get done around the house. You can also ask if the child spends a lot of time in a daycare situation. That's not to say that all day care places allow them to watch multiple cartoons and fairy tales. But it's possible. A better way might be to ask the child a few of your own questions such as: what do you like to watch on TV? Can you sing some of the songs you hear on TV for me? Do you watch shows with magic and angels and things?

Sometimes I feel like Sneaky Pete when I venture down this path, but I hide, quite successfully, behind the *in the interests of research* excuse. You can learn quite a bit with this sort of detective work. Of course, if during this Q&A session, you're told all about the last episode of Days of our Lives or Dr. Phil, or Ghost Whisperer–well, that's a hurdle of another kind, and you can be pretty sure that this child has a wild well of information inside that little head waiting to be shared. That's when you bring out the pencil and strike through that fascinating story you just heard about a ghost with red eyes down by the wading pool in the park with a machine gun.

The minds of young children are blank sheets of paper. Anything can be written on them and very often is. Unlike paper, they're also like sponges, soaking up everything they see and hear. They may not be able to make much sense of a lot of the stuff that's out there, but the more vivid images will stick. They retain them, building on them, just the way we do sometimes, and bring them out when they think the time's right.

Most importantly, use your instincts and discernment whenever you venture down this path, keeping in mind that it's possible that the child has been in the presence of someone who may have been obsessed with talking about death. Someone who may be unable to let go of a friend or relative's untimely death, perhaps; something that might cause the child to start obsessing too. Passing hearsay, on the other hand, is unlikely to leave an impression on a normally active young child.

Many years ago, on a visit to a nearby playground with my own children who were very young, I met a little girl who opened a conversation with me, out of the blue, that started with, *"I am sooo scared of the devil!"* Her eyes were as round as saucers and her hands were nervously clasping and unclasping, her fingers twisting and turning as she looked around the playground as though expecting something horrific to crawl out from behind the bushes or the swing set and grab her.

When I asked, "What devil?"

She said, "You know! *The Devil!*" She cupped her hand around her mouth and motioned me to bend my head. "The one with a pointy tail, an' a long fork he kin stab you with," she whispered.

"How old are you," I asked.

"I'm six!" She held up six fingers in case I didn't get it– or more likely, to show me she could count.

"Where did you hear about this Devil?" I asked.

"My mom. She says he's mean and nasty and he'll get me if I'm bad. So, I have to hide when I'm bad so he won't find me." Her eyes roamed the playground as she spoke.

"Where do you hide?"

"Under the stairs. But you mustn't tell anyone. He can hear everything." She put her fingers to her lips. "He scares me *sooo* much!" She swiveled on one foot, then, "Hi, Mommy!" She suddenly flung out an arm and pointed in the direction of the slide. "That's my mom over there with my baby brother!" In the way that kids do, she changed the subject with lightning speed.

I looked up and noticed a young woman standing at the bottom of the slide clapping her hands as a toddler came streaking down the steel curve and landed with a plop at her feet.

"Your mom told you about his devil?" I probed. "Did you see it on TV?"

"Na, unh. My mom always says, I gotta be good, OR ELSE!"

"Or else what?"

"He's gonna get me. I get scared when she tells me that."

My primitive first instinct was to tell her that was nonsense! And hike off to give her mom a tongue lashing for scaring a little child! But thankfully my judgmental self took a step back and I offered her a suggestion instead.

"Well, I have an idea." Watching my own children out of the corner of my eye, I took the plunge, "What if I leave a beautiful angel here with you to take care of you and chase that devil away?"

She stared at me trying to gauge what I'd said, for a moment, then nodded and asked, "Where'd you get a angel?"

"Oh, they're around, they come when you call them."

"Can I call one?"

"Sure. Just close your eyes, very tight, and imagine the most beautiful angel you can. An angel, all dressed up in a sparkly dress."

"Pink! A pink dress," she said. Her eyes were squeezed shut. "With stars!"

"Good choice."

"An' a wand!" She picked up a twig and waved it about laughing. "Look, I'm magic! You can make a wish if you like."

"Okay, here's my wish, so listen carefully. I wish that every time you get scared of this devil—or something mean and bad, all you have to do is think of your angel in her pink dress, and whatever's scaring you will vanish like magic!"

"Yup, she's got a wand!" She waved her arm in the air waving an imaginary wand. "'An' when she wants to turn you into something else she does like this and lo and behold! You're a toad!"

"Not this angel," I laughed. "This angel brings good things to people and chases away scary thoughts–and toads," I said. Out of the corner of my eye I saw one of my own children picking himself up out of the dirt, having tripped and fallen face down in the sandbox. I leaned down to the little girl and said, "I have to go now, but don't forget, you're never going to be scared of that Devil again because all you have to do is think of the pink angel and she'll be there to help. Okay?"

She opened her eyes and nodded seriously, "Okay."

~

Why you wonder, would a mother do such a thing? Not only was she using her religious beliefs and fear to control the child, she was reinforcing and continuing a very bad myth that should have been burned to ashes centuries ago. This was a particularly sensitive child, with an active and vivid imagination; one that could internalize the fearful images she was being fed, making her very afraid of a lot of bad make believe.

My guess is that it's usually not because the mother is an evil monster; it's that she's simply repeating what she has been taught and is unlikely to change her methods. With any luck, this child of a more progressive generation would be able to shed some of her mother's ideas, but it's hard not to believe everything your mother teaches you.

It occurred to me that I had probably interfered with someone else's ideas of parenting by bringing an Angel into the conversation, but I can't say it bothered me much. In fact, I hoped the little girl would introduce her into her mom's life one day.

~

When I'm talking to children about anything even mildly supernatural, I try to remember that anything even slightly mystical is fascinating, real and natural to them. They already believe in magic, good fairies and wicked witches, Rumplestilzskin and dragons. They've sat glued to movie screens, TVs and story books, listening to every word of the tales of beautiful princesses, handsome princes and Evil Queens and monsters. They're all a part of their lives; fairies, goblins and every other character their bedtime stories are peopled with. Not for one minute would I advocate that this wealth of childhood fantasy be done away with. Like everything else, it provides endless, colorful, happily ever after dreams and wishes, and should not be spared. Even an occasional witch has value, in that it has the added value of teaching a child that not everyone they meet is necessarily a good person.

So, it follows that angels and devils, are real to them too. They're as real, as real can be, and as you know, it's a bit of a tightrope trying to keep the fairy godmothers real and the ogres make-believe. But we try.

In looking for the truth from a child, open-mindedness, with a firm foothold in reality, are essential.

Chapter 19: Mark

The little boy pulled at his teacher's skirt.

"Someone was in my room las' night," he whispered.

"Mark, I asked you a question. Did you hear me?"

The little boy shuffled his feet under the desk and lowered his head. He didn't answer. His third grade teacher tried again. "Mark? Look at your book. Who won the race—was it the tortoise or the hare?" She grimaced. The child had been off in another world all morning.

Mark clasped his hands together under the desk and whispered, "The tortoise."

"That's right." She said, just as the school bell rang down the hallway. Class was over, it was Friday afternoon and the weekend couldn't come soon enough. She was ready to go home, ready for the weekend, late sleep-in mornings and Sunday all day at the beach with friends. "Okay, everyone, put your art work in your totes and form two lines—bus line and car line . . . What is it Mark?" The little boy who had seemed so distracted all morning was pulling at her skirt. "What do you want?" It was hard to disguise the impatience she felt.

"Someone was in my room las' night." He said. His eyes were open wide and his bottom lip quivered.

"Who was in your room? Was it your Mom? Or your Dad?"

He shook his head and shrugged. "No. It was someone I don't know." His eyes were big and troubled. He had his teacher's attention.

"What did the person look like? Was it a girl or a boy?"

"I think it was a boy—a big boy."

"Did you tell your mom?"

"My mom said 'GO TO SLEEP' . . . but I was too scared."

The teacher held on to Mark's arm and turned to the class. "Okay, everyone! Jason, get your sweater—it's hanging on your peg. Mark, do you want me to call your mom and tell her something in your room is making you scared?"

Mark nodded.

"Okay. Go get your tote now and get in line and I'll talk to your mom." The teacher shook her head, wondering what was going on with the little boy, as she watched the seven year old grab his backpack off the floor and plod to the door.

She was trained to recognize the signs of unusual behavior that might point to situations in a child's life, and what Mark had said didn't feel quite right to her. Who was the "Big boy" in his room? She made a mental note to call Mark's mother that night. Maybe it was nothing to worry about.

She picked up a small raincoat that had been left behind by one of the other children, folding it as she walked to her desk, thinking she'd call Mark's folks after dinner and make them aware of what the boy had said. She was certain it could all be cleared up once they knew about it. It was probably an older relative or a guest who had wandered into the wrong room.

But even as the thought entered her mind, her intuition was saying it didn't ring quite true. The child was scared of something.

"It's funny you should mention that," Mark's mother said when his teacher called. "It must have been after ten when he called me to come to his bedroom. Jordan, that's his older brother, was sound asleep and Mark was telling me something about this person who came into the room and gave Jordan a kiss on the cheek as if to say 'good night'. "

"Well, something or someone definitely scared Mark," the teacher said.

"What exactly did he say?" His mother asked. "How did he express it?"

"Come to think of it, he seemed to be distracted all morning, and I could tell that his mind was on something other than class. You know, he stared out of the window a lot. In fact twice, I asked him what he was looking at, and he just said, 'Nothing.' But then, after school he came and told me something about this 'big boy' in his room . . . I wondered if an older child might be teasing him or if he'd seen something on TV that might have scared him?"

"Well, he does have an older brother," the mother sounded puzzled. "But I haven't heard any teasing going on. Jordan is usually involved with his after-school activities, or off and riding his bike around the neighborhood. In fact, I wish he'd spend more time with Mark."

"Could there be a child in the neighborhood that he's afraid of? Or maybe there's someone at school? Has he ever mentioned—?"

The mother cut her off in mid-sentence. "No, I don't think so. Mark's very imaginative you know. In fact I think his imagination keeps him up until all hours. Space ships, monsters—he stays awake long after his brother has gone to sleep—like last night.

"And you and her dad and his brother were the only other people in the house?"

"Yes. My husband was lying in bed watching the news. I was just getting out of the shower when I heard Mark calling me."

"Did Mark describe what the person looked like?"

"This is crazy. There was no one there—but yes, he said it looked like a 'bright' and shiny person." She sounded flustered. "I'm almost embarrassed to be talking about this!"

The teacher laughed. "Don't be–you never know what they're going to come up with."

"Okay, I'm sure you hear a lot of stuff! Are you ready for this? Mark said this guy–this big boy, person, whoever, had lights on him that made him shine–those were his words. He said the light didn't hurt his eyes and that it moved slowly like it was floating, and then it looked at Mark. I can't believe I'm telling you this! It's so silly! The only thing I can think of was that it was some sort of shadow moving in front of their night light. But they were the only ones in the room!"

"What else did Mark say?" the teacher asked, hoping that the mother wouldn't cut her off.

"That this person felt like a nice person, but it made him afraid. He pulled the sheet up over his head so just his eyes were sticking out, and yelled for me."

"Has he done this before?" The teacher asked.

"No, not that I can think of . . . surely I would have remembered." The mother replied.

"I'm sure it's nothing. Maybe if you encourage him to talk about it–would that get it out of his head?"

"I'll think about it. Maybe ask if the person had a name."

"Hmmm. I'll let you know if he says anything more about it in class."

Mark didn't share anymore of the incident at school and his mother never contacted his teacher to tell her whether or not she had been able to find out anymore. It remained a mystery.

~

What do you think? Could it have been someone in spirit? A spirit guide or an Angel perhaps? The one thing I'm sure of is that whoever it was, it was light, and bright and gentle. There was no monster walking around Mark's bedroom in the middle of the night.

But I wondered why a spirit, supposedly a light and gentle spirit, would do that. Surely they know that such an appearance might be frightening to this child? Was this a *tactless* spirit? A spirit who just didn't think things through? They tell us that we keep our personalities when we cross over to the Other Side, so perhaps, even knowing that 'all things will be made clear to us', we shouldn't expect those who have passed on to magically become perfect beings–

anymore than we will be all-perfect beings when the time comes. What do you think?

Chapter 20: Mariella

Note: Mariella is one of the most open children I met, as you will see.

It was one of those quiet times when Rosalie settled herself in a corner of the couch as she did every evening at this time. It was almost time for eighteen month old Mariella to go to bed. Her eyes were beginning to droop as she lay comfortably on her mother's lap taking the last bottle of the day.

Rosalie knew this last bottle was going to have to go, but it made it so easy to lull the baby to sleep that she had held on to it almost as tightly as did Mariella. The child never took more than a few sips before she dozed off, so it really wasn't doing any harm, she reasoned. She nuzzled the soft crown of dark brown hair breathing in the sweet scent of baby shampoo. The sounds of children playing in the street, and garage doors opening and closing as parents came home from work, drifted through the open window.

After a while, she gently picked up the baby's small hand and let it lie limply in hers. She was almost asleep. Rosalie let her head drop back on the headrest of her chair and breathed deeply. She rested for a few moments, gauging the time before she could put the bottle aside and carry the little girl to bed without waking her.

She closed her eyes for a moment and as she did so, she was suddenly overcome with the distinct feeling that someone else was in the room with them. It was an almost tangible certainty. The strange feeling didn't frighten her. She recognized the sensation immediately because this had happened before.

She kept her eyes closed, leaned her head back and whispered, "Is that you, Papa?"

"I could feel him so strongly–over by the door," she said. "Of course there was no one there because he passed away nearly a year ago. And as I sat there, loving the feeling of having him near, but feeling like I was going to cry, I suddenly got the urge to sing the children's song, "Se Va la Lancha." (There Goes the Boat). It was a song that my Peruvian father had taught me as a child, a song I'd thought about often since he'd died, and I knew–don't ask me how–that he liked to hear me sing it to Mariella. He had planted it in my head.

So I began to sing softly and as I did, Mariella's eyes fluttered open. She turned her head sleepily, and as I sang, she pointed at the door and smiled. This was exactly where

I had felt my dad's presence. I sang the song several times and when I was finished, I asked her, "Who can you see? Is it *Abuelo*?' That, by the way, is Spanish for 'grandfather', and she immediately fixed her eyes on the closed door. "Show me again," I said, and she again pointed to the door.

Several weeks later, the scene was repeated, except that this time, Mariella hadn't been on the edge of sleep. She had seemed restless after her bottle and had pushed it away when her mother tried to get her to finish it. So Rosalie put her down on the floor and gave her a soft cover book to look at. She didn't want the book either; or Bom Bom the elephant, or the bear. She didn't want any of the toys that Rosalie tried to distract her with, so she turned on the TV. That didn't work either. Instead, Mariella pulled herself up on the chair arm and just stood there for a few moments, staring at the door.

Then slowly, putting one foot in front of the other, she walked towards it. Rosalie watched in fascination as she toddled across the room and, upon reaching the door, the baby knocked very gently and then turned around with a huge smile on her face, clapped her hands and ran back to her mother.

"Trying to keep it light, I asked who was there. I said, 'Is it Pedro (her stuffed rabbit,) is it Miggy? The penguin. Is it Gigi (the little girl next door?)' She shook her head vigorously, clearly frustrated with me. So I said, 'Is it *Abuelo?*' She smiled and nodded. And as she did so, I heard the name "Elias" mentioned on TV. Someone on TV speaking to someone named "Elias"! That was my dad's given name!"

"I knew absolutely, that her grandfather was here in the room with us, near the door, again." She said. "I don't need anyone to tell me it was or it wasn't, I KNOW it was. It's something I can't explain. I just KNOW!"

~

Two years later, something else happened. Rosalie was standing in the living room of the family's newly renovated home, admiring the results of months of planning and rebuilding.

"It had been my dad's idea to do the renovations and he gave us lots of ideas and was as excited as we were when the job finally got underway. He was a great visionary, very creative, and he seemed to have a special knack of anticipating the needs of our growing family. My husband and I implemented nearly all of his ideas, but unfortunately, he died before the work was finished and never got to see the finished product. That made me sad, but I found myself wondering if he really was close by, as Mariella and I seemed to think, and had he been watching us all the time? I wondered now if he was actually in the room with me, admiring the work."

She paused for a moment, and then she said, "Well, within seconds of that thought entering my mind, Mariella, who was busy eating a snack, took off running at full speed down the hallway to my bedroom. 'Where are you going?' I called after her, and she yelled something and was back in a flash, clutching a picture of my father that had been on my nightstand. It was the first time, to my knowledge, that she had ever touched the picture. 'Abuelo!' she cried joyously.

I guess I got my answer! Dad was in the room, looking things over and–the funny thing was, I could feel 'approval' all around that thought–if that makes any sense. I just knew that he liked how everything had turned out. I could practically see the creases on his face, his smile–I could feel his whole demeanor and it was one of pleasure. He was approving the great job we had done."

"Then there was the time not long after our second child, a son, was born when Mariella came running in from

191

the swing set where she had been entertaining herself while I attended to the baby, and said, 'I want to send Grandma a message.' She was breathless and perspiring as she flipped a strand of hair off her cheek.

'Sure,' I said, 'You want to call her? Send a video message? How do you want to do that?' Her grandmother lived in the next town to us, maybe thirty miles away. 'Shall we make a video message?'

She nodded and clapped her hands as I dug my phone out. "Go stand over there by the bookcase,' I told her, and smiled as she posed with one hand on her hip. "That's great. What do you want to say?' I asked as I began to video. 'What message do you want to give her?'

She answered me with one word, *'Elias.'* Well, Mariella doesn't normally go around saying the name 'Elias'–ever and she caught me completely caught off-guard. Is that the whole message?' I asked.

'Yes!' she answered, and before I could say another word, she turned, waved at the phone yelled, 'Bye, bye Grandma!' and ran back outside to play.

Where did she go? Was her grandfather outside? Did Mariella run back into the yard to tell him she'd delivered his message to her grandmother?

"And here's another thing, on a completely different note," Rosalie said, "Well not totally different, I suppose. But about six months ago, Mariella and I were in the car, driving home from the store when she began pleading with me to 'Stop the car!' I told her this wasn't a good place and asked her why she wanted to stop, she said, 'So the lady can get in and ride with us.'

"What lady?" I couldn't see anyone on the side of the road, behind or in front of us.

'Just stop, Mama! She wants us to stop!'

"Here we go again, I thought, and, not wanting to ignore her I stopped the car at the next stop light and waited until the light turned green. Then I asked, "Is the lady in?" She answered 'Yes,' so I began to ask questions. I found out that she was a nice lady and her name was Nellie. And Nellie was sitting right beside Mariella. The fact that Nellie was also colored blue was a bit unnerving. But I took a deep breath and said as calmly as I could, 'Let me know when she wants to get out.'

'She doesn't want to get out, Mama. She's coming home with us.'

"'Mariella had never done anything like that before," Rosalie said. "And I wasn't sure what to do, so, the blue lady came home with us, and thank goodness, that was the last I heard about her. I mean, even to someone as willing to listen as I am, this was weird! "

~

It had been over a year since I last heard from Rosalie, but out of the blue one night, the phone rang and there she was, with a brand new story for me.

"Mariella's five years old now," she told me, "and I thought we'd heard the last of her adventures into all these various dimensions she lives on. I hadn't heard anything from her for ages, so what she said made me sit up and say 'Ah ha!' I had just decided she was growing up and getting away from it all. On the other hand I was busy with our two year old son—you know how that goes, and Mariella was dealing with sharing the limelight with a new baby, now a toddler, so she probably had less time for her other worldly sorties."

"Then," Rosalie continued, "towards the middle of last year a major health scare brought me back to earth with a thump, taking over a big part of my life. It was very stressful for a while. It was a life-threatening situation, where my attention wasn't so much focused on Mariella's life as it was on mine, so I could easily have missed some things." She took a deep breath. "But here we go again!"

The month of February had been very cold. Everyone was feeling cooped up until one day, right in between snowstorms and ice pellets, the sun came out for a few days, and warmed things up. It dried up the mud puddles and sidewalks and one afternoon after school, Mariella asked if she could take her chalks and go out and draw on the concrete.

"I don't know how long she was out there," Rosalie said, "it must have been an hour or so. I was busy with the baby, but I'd been watching her out of the window and she was so totally engrossed in her coloring, and it was such a nice day, that I left her to play so I could get some things done.

I'd just put her brother in his swing chair when she came bursting through the door yelling for me to 'Come and see!'

'See what?' I asked. I had a dryer full of clothes I needed to fold and dinner to think about, so this wasn't the best time in the world for a break.

'Jus' come look! I've got a report for you!' Her hair was tangled and her cheeks were pink. Her fingers were dusty green and yellow from the chalk. Her eyes were bright with anticipation.

"What report?" I asked wondering what on earth could be so important that it couldn't wait. Her spirits fell and her eyes clouded over. "Okay, okay! I'll come! Stop pulling my sweater, Mariella! You'll stretch it."

Rosalie followed the little girl through the front door, holding her hand as they walked outside. Then she shook her mother's hand away and skipped over the grass to her drawings. 'Over here!' She said.

"I walked over to her art work," Rosalie said, "and when I got there I noticed that she had written something in the middle of her random coloring."

'A report for you, Mama!' She said excitedly, pointing at the collage, with one hand on her hip and beaming.

"There was a cool wind blowing the fine chalk dust across the cement and raising goose bumps on my arms even though I was wearing a sweater. Or was it something else . . ."

Rosalie stood there, hugging her arms and staring at the words in amazement. "I couldn't believe my eyes; there in carefully formed letters Mariella had written in chalk, YOU ARE HEALTHY. GO AND HAVE FUN.

"Oh, Mariella! I said. My eyes filled with tears and I began to cry.

Then she said, 'don't cry, Mama! It means you're not sick anymore!'

"I know, baby . . ." I said. I was staring at the word my daughter had written underneath the message. PURO and I could hardly speak.. It was signed by my father! That was my father's signature! He loved his cigars—and the word PURO is the Peruvian slang for cigar"

Rosalie was quiet for a moment, then she said to me, "We had agreed, before he died, that he would use that word 'PURO' to communicate with me from the Other Side."

I could hear the emotion in her voice as she spoke. "That slang word for 'cigar' is not in common usage and I'm absolutely certain Mariella has never heard it before. That message was from my dad!"

~

She was in no doubt. What a message of hope from someone who loved her still from across dimensions, and wanted to reassure her that she was healthy after a horrible scare. All I can say is that this family's is in for a fun ride with their daughter's invisible friends!

It's a great privilege to be allowed into a child's world of spirits and I am in no doubt that that's who she was seeing and playing with, and picking up on the side of the road.

The veil between our world and the hereafter is very thin in childhood and children are very clear channels. Spirits, often on the look-out for clear channels, are quick to recognize that they make wonderful messengers.

Mariella's mother, with her easy acceptance of the little girl's stories, has created a friendly climate where the opportunity for a glimpse into that seldom seen world of childhood can grow and flourish. They are both in a place that they can explore together without fear.

~

If you're interested in exploring these invisible worlds with a child, it's important to listen to what they're saying. And if you're lucky, you may find yourself in the right place at the right time to eavesdrop on one-sided conversations the child is having supposedly all by herself. Chances are, you know whoever's there, so this could also be the time to say something like, "Who's there? Can you see someone?" You might get a nod, a one word answer or a whole sentence. On the other hand, the youngster may decide to tell you nothing. This doesn't mean he or she is holding anything back–they may just not be in the mood to talk. But if they are, there's a mountain of information ready to erupt.

I believe that spirits appear to children just as they last saw them on the Other Side. It's natural, and probably commonplace, occurrence for them, so it's easy to see why they don't engage you in every visit with excitement or enthusiasm. These are normal friends that they are very familiar with, and the child may just assume that you can see them too. Which is why it's confusing to them when they're told they're imagining things.

...as it is in Heaven

Chapter 21: Candace

"No! She's not in Heaven! I've seen her!"

A four year old I met, named Candace, had her family turned upside down one evening when she became distraught at bedtime and began crying inconsolably, saying she wanted her Aunt Patty. No amount of cajoling would help, and picking up the phone and asking Aunt Patty to drop by, wasn't an option because she had died a year or so before the incident.

"I couldn't do a thing with her," Candace's mother said. "She kicked and squirmed away from me, lay on her back in the middle of the living room drumming her heels on the floor and saying she didn't want to go to bed, she was too sad and she wanted her Aunt and nobody else. It was especially weird because Candace hadn't really spent that much time with Patty when she was alive, so what was going on? I didn't know whether to feel hurt or mad!

I was also frustrated. It had been a long day and I was looking forward to reading the children a short bedtime story and getting some peace and quiet.

"So I said, 'Come along, Candace,' in my best Mommy voice, trying to keep the adult in me front and center, while fighting the urge to join her kicking and screaming on the floor. When she refused, I picked her up and carried her to her room, dodging her hysterical flailing as best I could. Once in the bedroom, she wrenched out of my arms and threw herself down on the bed, burying her face in the pillow, beating the mattress with her fists. She was crying so hard, her little face was crumpled, red and sweaty, and her hair clung in damp strands around her face. I didn't know what to do. So I yelled for my husband."

~

Try as they might, neither parent could comfort her.

"We told her that Aunt Patty was in Heaven with Jesus," her mother said, "and that we'd all see her one day, thinking that would calm her down, but she just cried harder and yelled "NO, SHE'S NOT! IN HEAVEN! I SEEN HER! WHY CAN'T I GO TO HER?"

Her little sister brought her toys and a favorite story book that she kicked out of the way while her dad just stood there helplessly with his hands on his hips. They'd never seen anything like this.

Candace's mom was at a loss. "Eventually, I just scooped her up and took her over to the rocking chair where I held her in a vice-like grip rocking like crazy until the hysterics stopped."

After what seemed like hours, the little girl finally cried herself out and fell asleep.

"Later, her dad and I just looked at each other, shook our heads and said, 'What was THAT about!'

"Patty was married to my mother's brother–and she died much too soon," Candace's mother explained as she told the story. "They didn't have any children, although Aunt Patty would have loved to have had a child but it just wasn't in the cards." She laughed sadly. "It wasn't in the cards! It wasn't in *our* deck of cards to lose Aunt Patty, so young!" She looked out of the window. "Funny I should say that . . . on one of the rare occasions when she and Candace were together, they played cards. They went from one game to another. Go Fish! Snap. You know, all those kid games. Patty never seemed to get bored and Candace loved it. Maybe that's was when the bond between them formed. They weren't close otherwise." She looked pensively at the floor. "I've been wondering ever since that night when she yelled, *'I've seen her!'* if Aunt Patty really did come to visit her."

So, the next morning, when the little girl got up and calmly sat down for breakfast at the kitchen table with her younger sister, and cheerfully attacked her bowl of Cheerios, her mother decided to ask her about it.

"Candace, last night when you were so upset, you were talking about Aunt Patty. You said you'd seen her?" She ventured nervously, hoping this wouldn't get her going again, "Do you remember?"

'Yup' the child said, taking a bite of the pop tart on her sister's tray, and was rewarded by the baby smacking her spoon into her milky cereal. 'Mom, look what Sissy did! She's splashing her milk and she got me wet!' Candace said, moving her plate further away from her younger sister.

It was as though the little girl had forgotten all about the drama of the night before and then she said, 'Aunt Patty has a big necklace.' She touched her fingers to her neck. 'And she's very big,' Candace spread both her arms as wide as she could, then spooned another mouthful of cereal into her mouth.

"What else," I asked her.

'She has a little dog. A little, white dog. She brought him to see me an' I wanted to hold it but she said 'not this time, Candace.' Oh, and she has purple nail polish on her toes and earrings.' A big smile lit up her face.

"Earrings on her toes?" I teased.

'Yup. Three green earrings on her toes!'

"I had no idea what she was talking about, but it sounded pretty fishy to me," her mother said. "So I decided to fish for more information. "I've never seen anyone wear earrings on their toes!"

'Aunt Patty does!'

"Are you sure?"

'Yeah, 'course! You 'member that day we ate those Cracker Jacks an' and we found little rings for toes in the box?'

I'd forgotten about that. "Oh, you mean *toe* rings! How could I have forgotten that?"

'But now Aunt Patty doesn't have to wear the Cracker Jack rings. Hers are green, an' pretty an' sparkly!' Candace added, nodded her head vigorously and reached for a piece of sliced apple. 'Not like those others.'

"Aunt Patty loved emeralds," her mother said. "Candace was making more sense than she knew. Patty was a raucously flamboyant dresser! So cheerful and jolly! *The more colors the better!'* She'd say as she swirled multi-colored scarves around her arm, draping them around my waist."

'And, remember you can never have enough Bling!' Candace interjected, making everyone laugh.

"That's the truth. Rhine stones flirted with real diamonds around Patty's neck, 14K chains dangled over her awesome bosom coupled with chunky crystals and glass beads. Her skirts were full and her trousers were fuller. Filled partly filled with Patty, and partly with yards of soft, brightly colored materials! What a character. But how did my daughter know that? She must've overheard something."

'Colors!' I remembered her saying once. 'Always wear lots of colors!' And, true to form, Patty's Christmas and birthday presents to us, when she was alive, were always liberally laced with all kinds of colorful, shiny bling–perky scarlet ankle socks, bright blue gloves in winter and floral everything!

When I asked my daughter if her aunt still had her scarves and beads, she said 'Yes—and lots of stuff for us to play with—girl stuff. We play girl things.' Blew me away!"

"But the funny thing was when she'd pushed her plate away, she just sat there thinking. And then she said, 'Her heart was beating very fast and it made her stop breathing—but she's all better now, Mommy.' And Candace smiled. 'She's in my room. She's painting her nails. Tell her I like hula hoops, Mommy! She's up there, now!'

I couldn't help grinning, and wondering, Why Candace? Why wasn't she communicating with me? Or with my mother who was her best friend?" She shook her head as she told the story. "I'm totally convinced that Candace wasn't making any of this up. She was so happy, it was contagious. I just said, 'You run on up and tell her you like hula hoops. And tell her I said 'Hi'!' I have to get Sissie ready for her play group."

~

Was Patty watching them all now? And was Candace, with her wide open mind, Patty's messenger?

Chapter 22: Frankie

"I dream of a dog just like her–"

And then there was the quiet little boy who lived at the beach. He was five years old, his name was Frankie, and he was having repetitive dreams about his Grandfather.

"It was really strange," his mother Samara confided. "The dreams began, as far as I can tell, about a year after his Grandpa died and they seem to happen often. At least every few weeks." She put her hand on her forehead. Her hair was the color of dark chocolate, about the same color as her eyes, and was cut close to her well-shaped head, in the style that many Caucasian women envied but few dared to try. "I'm thinking that they began around the time we moved here to Mississippi from Baton Rouge."

It was early evening and the sun was right at eye level making her squint as she remembered. Small gold earrings pierced her ears in two or three places, pinpricks of light against the dark bronze of her almost flawless skin.

She pursed her lips. I can tell you," she said, "there've been times when I've been tempted to find a therapist for that child, but here's the thing–I'm positive he's not making this stuff up, and he doesn't seem to be even a little bit upset by it. It makes no sense to me, but someone told me about you and the books you've written and I decided to call you and see if you can tell me what's going on."

The first time Frankie's parents heard about his dreams was one summer afternoon when the family had gone down to the beach to swim and roast hot dogs. "The kids love it and it's good for us to all be together. Plus, it fills up these long summer evenings," Samara said.

The day was warm and sunny, the wind was up, flicking the tops of the waves, sending spray high into the air, white capping the ocean far beyond the shore. She and her husband were sitting at the edge of the water watching their three young children splash in the waves as they raced up the beach, painting the sand with swirls of foam.

"Frankie was five, Lashane was four and Jessie was almost three." Samara said. "It was such a great day and I remember we smiled at each other feeling so lucky to have three healthy children and the beach, and the sunshine. We could hear the kids squealing and laughing when the cold water raced over their feet, making them jump out of the way. Life was good! And then it happened. Life was just about to get woo-woo weird!"

"All of a sudden, from a short way down the beach, a dog broke away from his leash and his owner, and came bounding towards the children. I remember thinking, Oh Lordy! I hope he's friendly! You know, he was one of those Rottweiler dogs? They can be scary. And then as I looked closer, I said to myself, not a 'he' that's a 'she'! That made me feel a little better."

The youngest child, frightened by the dog, ran towards her parents crying, but the dog was there to play and Frankie, and his younger brother were thrilled with their new playmate. They chased her, she chased them, and she ran this way and that, skillfully dodging their attempts to catch her. The boys threw sticks for her and yelled at her to "Catch!" They splashed her, and she snapped at the drops of water, and pounced on bunches of bubble weed making the children laugh.

"And then Frankie said the weirdest thing. He looked over at us and yelled, 'She always does that!' And took off after the dog and they went chasing into the sea together! Then they bounded out of the water and Frankie began tossing that seaweed up in the air for her again, making the dog jump and snatch it out of the air, and I heard him shout to his brother, 'She told me she likes the noise the bubbles make!'

"What was he talking about? Frankie had never seen this dog before! But I dismissed the thought. I couldn't tell who was having more fun, the dog or the children," Samara said. "I told my husband Jackson that the dog must still be a pup. She wasn't that big and I've never seen so much energy!"

Samara let her mind wander back over that afternoon at the beach, remembering.

"It's good for the boys," her husband Jackson had replied as he heaved himself up from his prone position under the umbrella to watch. "Every boy needs a dog."

"Or every dog needs a boy, by the looks of things!" his wife laughed.

"I had a lot of fun with mine." He looked pensively over the tops of his sun glasses and didn't say anything for a moment. Then, "In fact that dog looks a lot like–"

"Watch this, Daddy!" Lashane yelled as he came scrambling across the sand with the dog in full pursuit, ears flopping, fur streaming in the breeze, as the child flung himself on the beach yelling, "SLIDE!" and the pup landed on top of him.

The little boy pulled himself out from under the mass of wet doggy hair, covered with sand and beaming. "Cool, huh!"

"Very cool," his dad laughed and watched the dog as it sneezed, then shook a coat full of salty water all over them. "WHOA!"

The dog stayed for no longer than about ten minutes, then, from somewhere down the beach, they could hear someone whistling. She stopped in mid stride, cocked her head to one side, spun around, kicking up a curtain of sand, and raced off down the beach to join the whistler.

"Ahhh! Where'd she go?" Frankie asked, staring down the beach.

"That's prob'ly her owner whistling," his mother said. "He probably wants her back on the leash so they can take her home."

Frankie squinted his eyes against the sun, raised his hands to shield them and said," I don't get it . . ."

The sun was riding low on the horizon by the time the family gathered around a small grill on the sand. Jackson was handing out hot dogs and Samara was helping the children to stick them on the ends of metal forks. A cardboard box lay on the sand close by with a bag of buns and shucked yellow corn. Beside it, was a bag of giant marshmallows, slabs of chocolate and sweet crackers.

The children sat by the and the forked "weenie dogs", as their youngest child called them, were sizzling. Lashane had already lost one pink wiener to a sandy grave.

"I wish that dog was still here," he said gazing hopefully down the beach. "She could've et the one that dropped."

"*Eat*. Don't you know the word's 'eat'? Doofus." Frankie remarked, quietly munching on a bag of chips, staring at the sea. "I dream of a dog like her," he said to no one in particular.

"Hand me that corn, Son," his mother said. "You dreamed of a dog like her?"

"Yes. I *dream* of her," he said seriously. His almost black, curly hair, wet from the sea, glinted in the still bright, setting sunlight. His eyes, big and brown like his mother's, held hers steadily. "An' she looks just like that dog we've bin playin' with."

"Did you dream of her more than once?" she asked, placing the corn cobs on the grill beside the wieners.

"Lottsa times. Every time I dream of Papaw he brings that dog."

His father stood quite still, listening to his son. "When did you dream of Papaw?"

"I dream of him alla time," said the little boy. "Do you, daddy?

"I think of Papaw a lot, boy, and sometimes I dream of him. I sure do miss that old man," Jackson ruffled the five year olds hair and gazed out over the sea.

"Do you dream of the dog, too?" Frankie said, holding out a pale pink, sticky palm for a second hot dog. "No bun! Just the weenydog," he told his mother.

His dad forked one of the sausages off the grill and handed it to him. "Can't say as I do, son."

"Papaw calls his dog 'Zelda'. He says, 'Fetch, Zelda!' and in the dream, I play catch with them. Jus' like today."

"And then Jessie asked me if she could have marshmallow, and we forgot about the dog." Samara said.

"But that night, when we were getting ready for bed, I noticed my husband staring at the watch he'd just taken off and placed on the dresser. 'Isn't that the one your daddy gave you? I asked him. And he said, 'Yes, it's the watch they gave the old man when he retired from the railroad after 30 years.'

I remembered that. Poor Jackson, I was thinking. I could feel his grief still, even though it had been eight years or more since he lost his daddy. "Funny, how Frankie said he dreams of him all the time," I said. "How would a year old child even remember him! I figured that's how old he was when Papaw died. How would he even know it's him?"

Jackson sat down on the side of the bed and pulled his sneakers off. "Un hunh . . ." He tugged at a shoelace, "What's funnier than that was when he talked about the dog on the beach looking just like the dog in his dream. Daddy's lifelong buddy was a Rottweiler, black and brown, just like that pup that they were playing with."

I didn't say anything. My husband's known as a big ol' quiet man among his friends. Know what I mean? He doesn't say too much but there are times when I know he's about to say something, and I know it's going to be important and I just listen.

"The dog's name was Zelda," he said. "Daddy figured that was a good German name for a Rottweiler."

Well, I almost died! "How did Frankie know that? He couldn't possibly have known that! That's just not possible, Jack!" I said.

"I know that. That pup died, an ol' dog, before I met you, Mama!"

"Wha . . ." I didn't know what to say, I just kept saying, Frankie couldn't possibly have known about the dog let alone its name." Samara just shook her head. "It's not even probable he remembered his grandfather, but that dog named Zelda died years before the child was born." She finished. "So, how can that be?"

~

When I asked Samara the question, "Samara do you believe people have eternal souls?"

She replied "Of course I do."

216

And when I asked, "What about animals, do you think they have souls?"

She said, "Well, now, I hadn't really thought about it."

"If you believe that Papaw has an eternal soul then isn't it possible Frankie really did see him? And if you believe as I do, that animals have souls too, doesn't it make sense that he would bring Zelda with him when he visits Frankie in his dreams?"

"I guess it could happen . . . Frankie's always loved dogs ever since he was a small child. Oh my, I have to think about all this."

~

I wonder what she would have thought if I'd told her that, in my universe, it was quite possible that all three of them, Frankie, Zelda and Papaw all knew each other on the Other Side? But maybe that was a discussion for another day

It's strange to me that some people don't believe that animals have souls or, like Samara, just haven't really thought about it. All they have to do is look into a dog's eyes. Look into the eyes of any animal. *Really* look. Cats leave you in no doubt as to their, somewhat picky little spirits. Chimpanzees almost speak to you through their eyes. They talk about eyes being the "Windows to the Soul", and in my opinion, there are no clearer windows than the eyes of an animal.

~

After my husband, Walter, transitioned to the Other Side, he would come into our dreams with a 'deceased' family dog at his side. In a dream that my youngest son Drew had, he told us that his dad was standing there talking to him about the amazing, 'out-of-this-world' computers they have in Heaven, and that Cassie, our lab who had died about two years before, was with him.

During a vision I had just before our son passed, I watched Walter as he came to help Drew over to the Other Side with Cassie at his side—with three of her still-born puppies.

So, yes, animals have spirits, and if Papaw was coming into Frankie's dreams, why wouldn't he bring his lifelong buddy with him. What a gift to his family.

Chapter 23: Martin, Gemma & Jason

Closer to Heaven

The long, curving corridor with its pale, marbled tile that ran the length of the Pediatric floor was quiet. The lights had been dimmed for the night and a young Resident was wrapping up his shift. His name was Jack Mackenzie. The children called him Doctor Jack. He placed his hands on the nurse's station desk and lowered his head.

"You look exhausted," the elderly nurse behind the desk commented. "Why don't you go lie down and get some sleep while you can. Something in my bones tells me this is going to be a difficult night."

Jack groaned. The nurse had been working here long before he arrived–long before I was born, probably, he thought, and word on the floor was that she had developed an uncanny sense of impending turmoil and bad things happening. Usually, unwanted complications and general havoc. He hadn't believed it when he'd eavesdropped on a late night conversation between two of the younger nurses, not long after he got here, but now, going into the end of his second year of residency he'd learned not to be skeptical when Nurse Collins made strange remarks.

"Just so long as it's not another mass food poisoning episode like the one following someone's tenth birthday party a few months ago." he told her.

She said, "Ummph! Get yourself out of here!" and flapped a magazine at him, shooing him away.

"I will. Right after I check 25," He yawned, "I'm so tired I can't even think straight." How pointless that sounded. Everyone was tired. He'd caught a first year intern sound asleep with her head down on the desk at the nurse's station not long ago. That was the week after the food poisoning gig, come to think about it.

He trundled off down the hall, hands swinging at his sides, head thrown back, knocked gently on the door to Martin's room and pushed it open gently. The bedside lamp was off, and the only light in the room came from the red and green lights on the monitors and a small night lamp on a stand in the corner beside the two-seater couch where the child's mother sat.

She pulled herself upright when the doctor entered. There were dark circles under her eyes and her hair was pulled back, clasped at the back of her neck, with wisps falling loosely on either side of her face.

"How's it going?" He asked. Stupid question, her five year old was in the final stages of a cancer that no one had found a way to stop. A Glio Blastoma that was fast consuming every ounce of the boy's energy, leaving him wasted and ravaged in its relentless spread. He checked his chart noting that tonight his breathing was ragged and more labored than it had been earlier in the evening.

"He's been asleep for about an hour, I think," his mother said flatly.

The young doctor lifted the child's arm, felt for a pulse then gently placed his wrist back on top of the covers. Turning away from the bed, he sat down beside the woman and took her hand. There was nothing to say. They had been waiting for this day and they both knew there wasn't going to be any last-minute miracle, no reprieve that Jack could see. Martin might survive the night, but he had his doubts.

The little boy's mother's eyes brimmed with tears. "Stay strong," He patted her hand and stood up to leave. "Would you like us to call his grandparents to keep you company?" The boy's father had been absent from the scene for months and Jack didn't expect him to show up now.

"It won't be long, will it?" Her eyes begged him for an answer–any answer other than the one she already knew.

"I can't tell you that for sure. I'm going to catch some sleep now, and I'd like to know there's someone with you. I'll be right down the hall if you need me."

She nodded, her eyes filled with tears and she whispered, "Thank you".

The young doctor walked towards the door and as he placed his hand on the knob, a small voice said, "Doctor Jack . . ."

"Marty! You awake, buddy?"

"Yeah," there was a faint smile on his lips. "I'm lookin' at clouds."

Jack looked towards the wide windows that looked out onto the park. The curtains were closed. "Where? Show me the clouds," he said, leaning down so he could hear the little boy's weak voice.

His mother left the couch and stood beside the bed stroking the child's hair. "Where baby? Show Mama and Doctor Jack."

"You knock . . . like this," The little boy raised his hand weakly, clenched his little fist, bruised from too many recent 1Vs, and made a knocking motion. "An' I said, 'Peter, Peter, let me come in! You knock an' he opens the door." The little boy struggled to take a breath.

"Peter opened the door?"

"Yes . . . An' shows me clouds–big white clouds. But you can't come, Mama–" His voice tapered off and he closed his eyes. "Don't worry, Mama . . . it's nice. Lights. With colors . . . I like the lights–so pretty. I like it here, but you can't come . . ." Martin's eye lids fluttered and were still.

Jack leaned closer. For long seconds, Martin didn't appear to be breathing. And then he took one shallow breath.

His mother let out a sob and put her hand to her mouth. "Did you hear that?"

As Jack reached for his stethoscope, the child took another breath. He watched as the air left his body; his chest sank slowly and almost imperceptibly and then it was over.

The room was quiet. No sound came from the monitors, the floor outside his room was quiet, and somewhere in the late evening the only sound was the faraway roar of a jet airplane taking off from the airport ten miles away. The only other sound in the room was the whisper of the air conditioning and the sharp intake of breath from the child's mother.

"Marty?" The intern felt for a pulse.

"Doctor Jack?" He heard the rising panic in the mother's voice.

"It's over," he said quietly, putting an arm around the mother to steady her as a deep, almost primeval sound escaped her lips. She swayed towards him, and he held her.

The charge nurse appeared in the doorway. "His grandparents are on the way, Doctor Mackenzie."

The mother pulled away and buried her head in the little boy's pillow and wept as the charge nurse hurried to her side. "He said there are lights–pretty colored lights," she whispered.

"Then there are," the nurse said gently.

~

Beautiful clouds . . . the young Resident scribbled on his chart, ran a hand through his hair and turned to the windows. Stepping towards them, he drew the curtains back and stared outside. There were no clouds to be seen here on earth tonight. "I guess he opened the door for you, little buddy." he said quietly.

~

Pediatricians, the parents of sick children, and more often, the nurses who work the pediatric floors in hospitals big and small, have seen these small miracles time and again.

We know that all young children seem to have direct lines to the afterlife, and no one knows that better than the people who care for them when they are either chronically ill or near death. Who and what are they seeing in those last days, hours or minutes of earthly life? Who's talking to them? Who's showing them pictures and sometimes, familiar faces? And who was the man called 'Peter' behind the closed door? All he had to do was knock.

~

My son dreamed one night that he and his father were sitting together in a small room, deep in a long conversation. I never had a chance to hear what they were discussing because Drew died suddenly a few days later. But, I'm willing to believe that his father's spirit was talking to his spirit in the dream; perhaps he was letting him know that his time on earth was soon to be over. Reminding him that this was the time he had chosen, long before he came to this dimension. Think so?

~

The grandmother of one young child tells the story of a little girl named Gemma who had been diagnosed with leukemia at two years old and had been in and out of hospitals for most of her six year old life. Most of those hospital stays had been at a big Virginia Medical center in her home town of Richmond, where the staff on the children's wing had gotten to know her well.

As it is with chronic illness, Gemma had good days and bad days, and when she was well enough it wasn't unusual to see her walking or being wheeled down the hallway, to visit another sick child who was too sick to get out of bed. She always had a bundle of books or a stuffed animal under her arm. She was a precocious little girl and learned to read early, probably as a result of being read to so much when she was bedridden. She liked to show off that talent by reading to the other children, but there was one thing she liked even more than that.

Late at night, when the hospital was quiet and the lights dimmed, the little girl would often have trouble sleeping. "I just can't keep my eyes shut," she'd tell her favorite nurse Abby. "Every time I try they just pop wide open!"

Whenever that happened, the nurse would say, "Okay, big girl! Let's go see if Johnny's on," and would help her into her chair, and wheel her down to the nurse's lounge. There was a big TV in there and plenty of comfy cushions that Abby could settle her into on one of the couches, patting the cushions this way and that, placing her teddy bears on either side of her, and turn on the program she liked best: The Johnny Carson Show. Sometimes they might have to wait for a few minutes for the show to begin or for a commercial to play out, but as soon as the familiar theme trumpeted out, Gemma would clap her hands and yell, *"Heeeer's* Johnny!!"

She would watch the show intently, only taking her eyes off the TV to sip from a mug of water the nurse placed at her side, or to talk about Doc's choice of clothing. She liked the animal segments. "Here comes Jack Hannah!" she'd announce. "Look Abby—he's got a squirrel thing—is that a squirrel?" And once she clapped her hand to her mouth, eyes wide, and said, "Oh no! That monkey peed on Johnny!" She giggled.

Towards the end of the show, her eyes would begin to droop, her little body would slump further down into the cushions, and she would fall asleep. Soon after, Abby would pick her up and carry her down the hall to bed.

One night, after a long day of tests and blood taking, Gemma was especially listless. Abby, came on the swing shift, checked her chart and walked down the hall to look in on her around supper time. She noted that the food on her tray was untouched. "Not hungry, Gemma?" she asked.

"Unh,unh."

"Not even a bite of chicken? A cracker?"

She shook her head.

"What if I go see if there's any jello in the refrigerator?"

228

The child shook her head, letting it roll to one side of the pillows.

"Okay. If you get hungry later, ask Molly for a cookie and some juice. Okay?"

Molly was the charge nurse that night. She would be working the night shift, relieving Abby at eleven.

"Where will you be?" Gemma asked in a small voice.

"I'll be going home later and Molly will be here to look after you."

"Why can't you look after me?" The child wanted to know.

"'Cos I'm going home to sleep," she smiled. "If you like I'll ask Molly to let you watch Johnny."

The child turned her head away. "When will you come back?"

"Tomorrow," Abby said cheerily. "I'll be here all day tomorrow." She was filling in for a day nurse who had called in sick. "You'll see me when you wake up. How about that!"

Gemma shook her head, 'No'.

She brightened her smile and tried again, "You'll see, I'll see you first thing in the morning."

"I won't see you . . ."

"'Course you will. Don't I always come when I say I will?"

"I won't be here," she said. "I'll be an angel in the morning."

~

The nurse found it difficult to sleep that night. She couldn't get Gemma's words out of her mind. She'd never said anything like that before. Maybe all the tests she'd been through recently had worn her out. Abby tossed and turned well into the night until she fell into a worried sleep and awoke with a start about two or three hours later. It was 3:00 a.m. She lay there for a while staring at the darkened ceiling willing herself to sleep but it was no good, so she heaved herself out of bed. If she couldn't go back to sleep she might as well go into work, she decided.

Trying not to wake her husband, she tiptoed out of the room and went into the bathroom down the hall to get dressed. Her eyes felt gritty and her stomach was queasy so she grabbed a banana out of a basket, shrugged into her coat and left the house.

There was no traffic at that hour of the morning so Abby made it to the hospital in record time and hurried through the revolving doors at the hospital entrance. She walked fast down the hall and took the elevator up to the ninth floor. Her stomach growled. A feeling of urgency made her hold her breath as she waited for the doors to open. She didn't know why. Her nerves must be on edge, she thought. Or maybe it was just a lack of sleep. Stepping out onto the floor, she walked down the hall towards the nurse's station where Molly was sitting at the desk, writing. The floor was quiet this early in the morning, and as she approached on soft-rubber-soled shoes, Molly raised her head. "Abby!"

She knew immediately, from the look on Molly's face that something was wrong. The charge nurse stood up and walked towards her. "Is it Gemma—"Abby asked.

"She's gone," Molly said quietly. "Gemma's gone . . ." She looked at Abby sadly, turned away from her and stepped back behind her desk. "At 2:59 this morning," she said glancing down at the log in front of her.

"She knew it would be tonight," Abby stared at the night nurse's notes. "She knew."

"Sometimes they do." Molly, who was nearing retirement, had heard that a few times before.

"Funny. I woke up at 3:00–a minute after. . . she knew!"

"Sometimes they do. We see and hear things like this time and again in patients whose time is near."

The old-fashioned turn of phrase Molly used was somehow comforting. Gemma's time had been near. It was just way too soon. Abby walked away as a wave of sadness overcame her, and then she smiled through her tears. Gemma could watch her friend Johnny very night from now on. Heck! She's probably met him already!

~

Mary Alice was a trauma nurse who worked on the pediatric floor of a large hospital in Houston, and had developed a special connection with a young man who had been in and out of the hospital, under her care, for the previous five years.

This didn't happen often in a trauma nurse's life whose work involved the care of critically ill children who, more often than not, never made it out of the emergency room, let alone the ICU unit.

Jason had come in, for the first time at the age of eleven, following a collapse on the gym floor. He was diagnosed with an inoperable brain tumor. It was a particularly aggressive cancer and it was treated as such, in the hopes that it might shrink enough to afford the boy a shot at a reasonably pain free life.

"For as long as we can give him anyway . . ." Mary Alice heard the oncologist say as he shrugged, knowing full well that this killer disease probably wouldn't give him much time for any sort of life. "Sometimes we get lucky and arrest the thing completely, but usually we don't. We just keep hoping, this will be the one. That's what keeps us doing this job. And kids like Jason," He smiled.

Sometimes the treatments worked and sometimes they didn't. But hope was kept alive by every day they managed to buy and sometimes there was actual improvement and the patient could be sent home. And every time there was a new crisis, the nursing staff readmitted him and attacked his cancer with renewed vehemence.

~

Jason was in and out of hospital on and off for the next several years and quickly got to be a favorite among the staff. Whenever Mary Alice heard he was back for another round, she'd come in the next morning with a fresh batch of toll house cookies she'd stayed up late to bake, knowing they were his favorite.

Then one summer's evening, he was brought into the emergency room, this time in worse condition than ever before.

In the hallway, outside the ICU, Mary Alice RN looked at her watch as she emerged from one of the children's rooms. Her shift was coming to an end and she was ready for a quiet evening at home with her husband and their two Scottie dogs. She sat down heavily in her swivel chair at the nurses' station to finish up her notes. It had been a long day.

The elevator door opened and she looked up and waved to the incoming nurse who had just arrived on duty, and as she did so, the phone rang at her elbow.

It was the ER with the news that Jason was on his way back to the unit. His condition was grave. The staff readied evening and the swing shift the room for his arrival. His doctor was on call that nurse, Mary Alice's relief, stood by the elevator as the boy was pushed through the doors and down through the hallway to the Pediatric ICU unit where Mary Alice waited.

He had lapsed into a non-responsive state. His vital signs were low and he would need all the help modern medicine could muster to pull through this one. The respiration unit was on standby in case his breathing worsened, IV's were hooked up and the heart monitor was turned on.

Mary Alice finished taping the last of the monitoring hook-ups to his chest. "There you go, Jason," She checked the IV on his wrist and placed his hand carefully at his side. "This'll make you feel better." She tucked the top sheet loosely around his body, noted his respiration and pulse rate on the chart and walked briskly outside to the nurse's station.

The boy's doctors were speaking to his parents at the end of the hallway, telling them that the tumor was resisting all treatment, it's growth had quickened and the drugs had stopped working.

"We've run out of options," the attending doctor was saying. "We hope that we can stabilize him tonight, but it's a long shot. This thing's just not going to be controlled." He ran a hand through his hair and glanced at the chart the nurse put in his hand. "He's in a coma now so is in no pain. That's the good news. If he should come out of it and regain consciousness, we can keep him pain free." He handed the chart back to the nurse and as quietly as he could, he said, "It's in God's hands now. We've done everything we can do."

Read, 'prepare yourselves for the worst,' Mary Alice thought.

"We'll pray," his father said.

"Yes, miracles happen!" His mother added, but the despair in her voice belied her brave words. "They do, don't they?" She whispered as her husband put his arm around her shoulders.

"All the time," he said. "Every day."

"Hold that thought," the oncologist put a hand on the man's shoulder and turned back to the desk as the parents walked down the hall to their son's room.

Mary Alice and the nurse who had just come on duty looked at the doctor, waiting for him to say something. "I'll be surprised if he survives the night," he said, holding out his hand for the chart, to record his orders. "Sometimes these things pick up speed, like Jason's has, and there's no slowing them down."

She had been about to call home and let her husband know that she'd be leaving the hospital soon, but instead, she changed her mind and decided to stay at work.

"Just get him settled in," she told her relief, "I'll come down and see him in a little while." Her voice was heavy. This wasn't completely unexpected. They all knew this day would come eventually, but she had become close to the boy. No matter how hard you try to keep your objectivity, there are times when this job gets very, very hard, she thought. "Sometimes I wonder why we do this." She said out loud.

"I know," was the quiet response. "Me too."

"Would you mind if I stayed a while?" Mary Alice asked.

"Stay as long as you like," the night nurse said. "I have a feeling this is going to be a long night, and your help would be welcome."

~

Twenty minutes later, Mary Alice made her way down the hallway to the boy's room and knocked softly on the half-open door and went inside.

She nodded to the youngster's parents and walked over to his bed. "Hi, Jason," she spoke softly and stood there watching him for a moment. "I know you may not hear me, but if you can, I just want you to know that I'll be here with you tonight." She smoothed his pillow, stroked his hair back from his forehead, glad he was in no more pain.

This disease was a monster. It had ravaged his young body, forced the kid into a life no teenager should have to endure. A life of pain, hospitals, drugs, surgeries, needles— and more pain. Her eyes filled with tears. It wasn't fair. "Cindy will be taking care of you tonight, but I'll be here on the floor checking on you."

She blinked hard and turned away from the bed. The boy's parents were sitting together on the couch in the corner of the unit and she put her hand his mother's shoulder. "You know Cindy–she's on duty tonight and she's one of the best," she forced a small smile. "He's in good hands. And I'll be just down the hall."

They nodded. And Mary Alice left the room.

Several times during the night she visited Jason, but there was no change in his condition. There was no visible movement in any of his extremities, no eye movement. The stimuli that they used with non-responsive patients, for checking tactile sensation in the patient, gave them a great big Nothing. Zero. He was hooked up to the respirator now, it's rasping push and pull of air, filling the room. Mary Alice could see that he was barely breathing on his own.

The oncology Resident came in during one of her visits "'Lo, Mary Alice," she said, picking up Jason's chart. "Still nothing?"

The nurse shook her head.

"The Glascow scale's showing a 3." The young doctor said glancing at the neurology notes. She moved to the boy's side and lifted each eyelid for any sign of cognizance–any sign of anything. But there was nothing. She checked the respirator beside the bed that was doing most of the breathing for him. "You know where to find me." She told Mary Alice. "I'll be right down the hall," she told the parents . "Cindy or Mary Alice will call if they need me for anything." She told them.

Jason's father stood up, and his mother said, "Glascow scale?"

"It's how we measure the depth of coma," the Resident answered. "A 3 means he's sleeping deeply right now." She reached up and put a hand on the father's arm. "I'm on the floor, if you need me, just call." She dropped her hand

and walked out, closing the door softly behind her. In fact, a 3 on the coma scale was as deep in coma as a patient could get, showing no evident response.

Midnight came and went. The night wore on, and as dawn began to lighten the hills outside the hospital windows, the parents approached the nurse's station where Mary and Cindy stood, to say they were going down to the restaurant to get some coffee.

"You'll call us, right? If there's any–change?" His mother said. Her face was drawn, there were sooty circles under her eyes, and her shoulders were slumped. Tears glinted from the hopeless darkness in her eyes and Mary Alice felt a lump like hard clay rising in her in throat.

Not Fair! She thought again. They were good people and they'd been dealt the worst hand any parent can get.

"You bet we will," she said. "Take your time, you need the break. They may have some cinnamon rolls just coming out of the oven about now. Gotta keep your strength up!" They looked like zombies she thought, as she walked with them to the elevators. It was a look they saw often on the Pediatric ICU floor in the wee small hours of dawn. "I'll stay with him until you get back," she told them.

They nodded wearily "You've all been so great," Jason's mother touched her arm. "Jason's been so lucky to have you all these years." All Mary Alice could do was nod as they stepped into the elevator, and watch the doors close behind them.

She walked back to the unit. It had been about two hours since she'd last been into Jason's room. Someone had drawn the curtains and left only one lamp on. Cindy, the night nurse was taking a snack break, and Mary Alice was alone with the boy

She stood beside him in silence for a few minutes, watching his chest rising and falling almost imperceptibly– nearly all of it machine-made movement. It wouldn't be long now, she thought.

She thought of her own son, almost the same age as Jason, and the thought was more than she wanted to cope with right now. Her heart was heavy as she stroked his arm before walking over to the couch to straighten the rugs and plump up the cushions. Not through any necessity, the action was more to keep herself moving and maintain her equilibrium in the face of the certain death of the boy–a child, really–one she had cared for and come to know over the years. How many times had she sat with him for a few moments at a time, looked in on him before she left for the day or to bring him a special treat from the kitchen? Her thoughts went to his last birthday that they had celebrated in the hospital with his family and friends. The confetti cake he asked for, the clown. . . Such a kid!

His parents were exhausted. From the initial diagnosis to now had been over five years. And as it usually does, this terrible disease had taken its toll on the whole family.

She opened the drapes slightly. The sky was beginning to lighten. It looked like a beautiful sunrise was brewing and for a moment, her mood lifted as she watched the rays of the sun shooting skywards, elevating the day. Then slowly, she drew the curtains closed behind her.

When she turned back to the bed, Mary Alice knew immediately that something had changed, and in an instant she knew what it was. Jason's had moved. It had been lying by his side just a few minutes ago, now his hand was on his thigh. For a moment she held her breath allowing herself to hope beyond all reasonable hope. And as she watched it, his finger twitched.

"Jason?" Her voice was a husky whisper.

"M'alice? His voice was weak, but his eyes were open.

"Jason!"

"Lights . . . so many lights . . . trees . . . so green, wow!" His lips moved slowly and with difficulty but his eyes were wide open and staring at something a long way past her.

She turned her head but there was nothing but the shadowy folds of the thick, closed drapes. She looked back at him. His eyes were still focused on whatever it was only he could see and there was a look of wonder in them. Had he seen the faint light of dawn when she cracked the drapes open? "Can you see the lights now, honey?"

In response she saw the look of wonder in his eyes as he reached for something only he could see.

Mary Alice pressed the call button and within seconds the desk answered. "Page Jason's folks–he's speaking." She returned the speaker to the wall.

"Jason, tell me what else you see."

"The ocean–it's *huge* . . . and blue . . . so blue–never seen so blue . . ." There seemed to be a faint smile on his lips as he paused, closed his eyes for a moment and said, ". . . the children–they're playing in the light . . ."

There were the sound of hurried footsteps in the hallway and the door to Jason's room swung open. "Jason!"

Both parents rushed to his bedside. "Jason!" His mother cried.

There was no answer. The young man was gone. His spirit had left, leaving behind the faintest smile on his lips.

"Oh, my baby! Jason!" His mother's words sounded as they were wrenched from the bottom of her soul. She stumbled as her husband steadied her and led her to the couch. *"My baby!* Oh Jason–why didn't you wait!" She cried, pulling away from her husband. She turned to Mary Alice, holding out her hands. "Why didn't he wait? He could have waited!"

The RN took both the mother's hands in hers. "That's the way it happens sometimes. It's easier for them." She said softly.

"What?"

She could have told the mother that very often, a person's spirit will choose that time to leave. That sometimes it's just too hard to go when the people they love the most are in the room. So, they wait until they've stepped out for a moment. Instead, Mary Alice said. "It was his choice to leave this way. It's easier."

"This happens? A person can really choose?" Jason's father asked. He looked up as Cindy walked into the room.

"We see it often," she said, and put a hand on the father's shoulder. "He's at peace now–that's what he wants you to remember."

The sound of the parent's grief filled the room; filled the empty space in and around the hospital bed that Jason had just left.

Mary Alice went over to his side and laid her hand on his chest. Tears blurred her eyes. Jason was in a wonderful light-filled place–with the children, beside the bluest ocean he'd ever seen.

"Play well, little man," she whispered. "I hope they have tollhouse cookies wherever you are." She turned and walked away closing the door behind her, leaving the parents alone with their son in the quiet of the darkened room.

Damn, damn, damn! Mary Alice grabbed her coat, punched the time clock and walked out of the hospital. Damn!

Chapter 24: I Had a Dream

"I don't know! It was weird.

I mean, why would my brain think up something like that?"

Children are wide open channels. It doesn't matter whether they're five or fifteen those open lines to other dimensions remain open, waiting to be tapped into. With younger children it happens almost spontaneously, as we have seen, and this might be because they are still so very close to The Other Side that their memories are fresh and uncluttered. It happens with older children too, but not as easily.

Please! Talk about un-cool! What do you suppose would happen, Ginny, if I told my friends in the seventh grade, that I can see ghosts? Duh! That's just stupid. Anyway, who says they're ghosts? Maybe I'm just plain crazy! Have you ever thought of *that?* I'm a nut!! Loony tunes! He thinks he can see ghosts! Ha! Ha! Hey you guys, crazy boy here thinks he can see ghosts! Wooo . . Woooo BOO! Ha ha!

Yup, you can see how that would go over. So, for the most, it's been my experience that the teen years are the time to put this stuff away until everyone grows up–and maybe that won't ever happen for some. So, dude. . . don't bring it up again! Ever. Sometimes some people never allow themselves to think out of the box or wonder 'what if?' So, keep quiet. Don't say a word about this crap or you'll be laughed out of town.

It's hard to find a teen who will open up to you about a strange dream or spirit encounter. And you know they can't be pushed. Try that and watch how fast those heels dig in, the brakes slam on, and everything comes to a grinding halt. You may as well give up.

Even Becca, my own little family mystic, began to close down when she and the sophistication of the ninth grade met face to face and found that they were on a collision course with all that whimsy. I still talk to her sometimes about spirits and signs and things that I think might catch her attention, and sometimes she yawns, and she might start to hum. That means 'I can't here you! Da-da-da-da-da-da!' But every so often, something grabs her interest and I get this mysterious little smile that I've interpreted to mean, 'Cool–let me think about.'

247

Occasionally, an older child may tell you about a dream he had, starting with "It was so weird!"

He's testing the waters. He's watching you closely, even though his eyes are glued to the pancake on his plate. Don't be fooled. You can be dead-eyed dick certain that if he thinks you're going to get weirded out by his dream, that will be all you'll get.

The teen age mind is in constant transition. Think back a few years and try to remember. A lot of weird things happen when you come to the rapids in this life river that will, eventually, lead you into adulthood. You stumble through the high water, slipping and sliding on rocks that have been tossed around to confuse you. Your reflection, grimacing back at you from the still, glass ponds in your bathroom mirror, is hard to recognize. Your nose has grown. You've got spots and there's this pale soft fuzz crap on your cheeks. Not to mention the curly-queues done below. Things keep changing. Every time you turn a corner it seems that there's another change lying in wait. Just as you get a handle on one thing, Blam! Something else comes up. Swirling waters play with your mind making it hard to know what to do next.

And now there are strange dreams being thrown into the mix. He doesn't want to think about this new complication. Sometimes the 'weirdness' is too weird to talk about–what if it should indict him in some way? What if it confirms beyond a doubt what he already feels–that he's different! And probably, stir crazy. He already feels pretty weird just thinking about it, so it may be best to say NOTHING! He knows exactly what his mom would say, "Everyone feels that way sometimes. Don't worry, you're perfectly normal!"

She just doesn't know. I'm not like everybody else! She'd probably tell me the dream's perfectly normal too. Well, here's a bulletin for you–it felt as though I was living and breathing in the dream, like I was *there!* A part of it. I was with all these strange people and goings on. It was that real! How can that be normal? So, I'll just put the thing back in whatever idiot box it came out of and forget about it. If anyone had even an inkling about what's going on, they'd start looking at me like I'm totally off the wall crazy.

Middle school's hard enough as it is without that.

~

As parents we have to ask ourselves, what if the comment that your teenager floated out there was floated in an effort to engage you? Could he be looking for an answer from you, his mom or dad, for some reassurance?

So, you find the right words and attempt to convince him that he's totally normal in every way. He's not cracking up. And even though he probably won't acknowledge it, he'll either feel better or decide you're even more naive than he thought. On some level, he might give you the benefit of the doubt and, in spite of himself, feel better, knowing that you think he's fine, and not at all weird.

If the door cracks open even a little, you might even be able to ask for more details of the dream—and he might surprise you. You could say something like, "Strange!" But on second thoughts, cross out the word 'strange'. He's already sure of that. Try instead, "What do you think it meant?"

"I don't know! It was weird. I mean, why would my brain come up with something like *that*?" He might cock his head on one side and screw up his eyes.

There's still room to press the advantage, so you do, and if you're very lucky he might tell you how real the dream felt and even ask you what you think. That's your cue to discuss it with him.

The discussion will probably be relatively short-lived, but don't read anything into this. It probably has nothing to do with you, it's just that he's a Middle-Schooler and now that it's been established that he's A-OK, neither psychotic nor bonkers, he wants to get out and get on with other things—like basket ball. And the pep rally in the gym, and quit worrying about stupid dreams.

But you know, and so do I, that the dream was one of those very real dreams that aren't really dreams, but visits—and on some level, he knows it too. And that's enough for now.

He's got plenty on his plate right now and doesn't need the distraction of other dimensions. The teen years will pass, as all years do, and one day, something may remind him of that dream—or some other weirdness he felt, and when the time's right, he may begin to explore the phenomenon.

Chapter 25: And another . . .

"Everything was so real—like I was living in it."

The following dream was given to me by a much younger child. And the difference was obvious. Although she had to be coaxed out of an unusual attack of shyness by her dad, when she began to talk, it was as though she was living it. There was no doubt in her mind, no wavering in her belief that, for a few moments of the night, the dream had been her stage and she was the leading lady.

Wendy was five years old when she had that dream. I heard it while visiting friends in California. It was early fall and I was sitting in the sunroom finishing my second cup of coffee, enjoying the sunshine when the little girl waddled towards me in a swirl of turquoise net and tulle with a lop-sided tiara perched on top of the nest of red, sleep-fuzzled hair. She was sucking the forefinger of one hand and clinging to her father with the other.

"Come on, Wendy," he said, "Let's hear about the dream again," he inched her forward and sat himself down in a chair opposite me with the child between his knees.

She leaned into him for just a moment as though she was deciding whether to deliver or not, and then, without warning, her face burst into a grin from ear to ear and she shoved off from her dad and took center stage.

She flung both arms up in the air. "I had this dream! I know it was just a dream, but everything was so *real* that I thought I was living right there inside it!"

"You did?" her dad interjected.

"'Course! What d'ya think?" she replied tartly. "I was inside it."

My ears perked up the way they do when I sense that something magic is about to be shared. And it wasn't the October sunshine reflecting the light off thousands of golden-yellow leaves clinging to the trembling Aspen in the front garden.

The child scooped up her Cinderella gown, adjusted her princess crown and heaved herself up onto the wicker couch beside me and whispered just loudly enough for me to hear, "I saw Uncle Pete last night." She said

"You did?" This wasn't what I'd expected! Her uncle, Pete to the rest of us, had died suddenly and tragically two years before.

"Yup," she acknowledged. "It was when I was walking in the forest. It was a very dark and big forest!" Her eyes grew round as she talked. "It got darker and darker an' scary and the trees were big with claws an' spikes an' everything an' there were giant—"

"Stick to the story, cut the theatrics," her dad admonished his little drama queen.

"Daddieee! " She frowned. "Okay, Well, it was very cold there, an' I kept walking and it got darker an' darker an' I didn't know how to get out and I got very scared . . ." Her hands reached up to her cheeks and she made an O with her mouth.

"That must have been really scary," I said.

"It was! I was really, really scared an' I didn't know where my mom was—or my dad—or my brothers and I began to cry 'cos it was really, really dark and I could hear sounds like legs chasing me."

"And what happened next?" I asked, trying to move her along.. This was a child who loved to perform, one who lived for every Kindergarten concert and Holiday Pageant where, as out-going a she was, she always managed to secure some pretty good speaking and dancing and singing roles. Right now, I didn't want her to scare herself right out of the story she was telling.

"I was cryin' and cryin' and I didn't know what to do and that's when I saw Uncle Pete. An' he was smiling. He was standing in a sunny place just smiling and he said, 'Hi Wendy! Are you lost? Come with me an' I'll show you the way.' He wasn't scary and the big scary trees were way back somewhere. I wasn't scared one bit anymore, so I went with him and we walked down the path. It was all sunny now–no more dark places. I held his hand and I was happy 'cos he showed me the way out of the forest. Where I could see my house and my mom again."

"And what did Uncle Pete do next?"

"Umm," she put her fingers on her chin as she tried to remember. Then she shrugged. "I think he went away. Maybe back into the forest?"

I shrugged. "Do you know where that forest is?" I asked. Have you ever seen it before?"

"Nope, I don't know where it is," She scrunched up her eyes as she thought.

I told her. "Maybe it was just a dream forest."

"Yes, a dream forest," she agreed. "I hope I don't see that forest again."

"That's a great dream, Wendy. I'm so glad you told me." I said. "I'm sorry you got scared though'. But Uncle Pete was there to help you find your way back home. Isn't that wonderful?"

The tiara tilted dangerously and she shoved it back up onto the crown of her head. "Yup. Ouch!" She scratched her head. "Daddy will you help me get this off? It's pulling my hair."

~

Of course Pete was there. Why wouldn't he be? He loved his nieces and nephews in life and I'm sure he still does. He loved being around them, playing with them, baby sitting them, and whatever they did together, you can be sure it was great fun.

This little girl was joyfully full of drama and brilliant imagination. Magnificent creativity goes hand and hand with those wonderful attributes. So, as I always say, Question Everything.

I did with this child. From the outset, I had no doubt that she had a dream about being lost in the forest or that her Uncle Pete came into the dream to show her the way out.

~

First you look at the obvious reasons for the dream. Obviously, a hundred small anxieties from the day before could have come together in her sub-conscious to produce a dream of being lost in the woods, with giant ugly trees trying to grab you. To invoke that sort of a dream scenario, all you have to do is watch Disney's Snow White. But Disney wasn't to blame in this case so that could be ruled out. But who knows what other triggers had trickled through her day and stuck in her sub-conscious? Some she may not even remember.

I had to wonder why Pete showed up after all these years. There had been no other dreams of him that anyone knew of, and the last time she saw her uncle was when they went skiing when she was about three. It turned out that Wendy wanted no part of the snow, the boots, the skis or anything to do with the icy slopes. Instead, she threw herself face down in the snow and bellowed until someone picked her up and took her back to the hotel.

You may be thinking, as I am, that it could have been Uncle Pete who rescued her from the slopes that day. He was there, and it's quite likely he would do something like that. I don't know, and I'm sure no one else would remember. But if so, a part of her brain might have retained that memory and, reinforced by the trauma of his passing, imprinted it and made a strong memory of someone who loved her and rescued her when she was scared.

That's one way it could have come about. Then you have to also ask, did she exaggerated the part about Pete? It's possible. With a lot of us, child or adult, the urge to exaggerate can be tempting.

Uncluttered minds, simplicity, and trust allow them to believe in fairy tales, to become one with Cinderella, Sleeping Beauty, the handsome princes and fabulous princesses. Tee that up with a vivid imagination and anything can happen.

On the other hand, if a child is having a nightmare, isn't it highly likely that she would wake up and run crying into her parents to be comforted? But in this case, it seems that Uncle Pete intervened, comforted her, allowing her to fall gently back asleep in her own bed.

My belief that most children are super-receptive to spirit connections is unshaken. It could very easily be as simple as that, in spirit, Pete visited his niece in a dream.

A lot of people would say, "Nah! Just a dream."

I'd say, you'd have to be there.

~

Then there are those on the other end of the imagination spectrum, the people who are analytical by nature, whose jobs or lives are dominated by the left brain and just find it more practical to rely on stratospheric math theories to solve problems. They would almost never be caught in a yoga class or mediation group. Any more than I would be caught dead trying to teach calculus or even 2 + 2.

It's not that they lack imagination. Of course not. They just find analyzing their engineering problems more exciting. Calculating the amount of fuel needed in a shuttle launch! What bliss!

I just want to know, 'What did you see when you were out there, thousands and thousands of miles above the earth?' Were there strange lights? Beings?

So why is it that some of the brainiest people we know, the researchers and dissectors of neuroscience, astrophysics, math, and psychology—brainy people, every one of them—very often dismissive of things that sound too fantastic or out-of-this-world?

They're just not thinking far enough in all directions, is what I think. It's a matter of focus too.

When they say that theories and personal accounts that are too ethereal or too non-substantive—like dreams or visions, I say phooey! Unleash those brains and just allow strange thoughts to appear. *Think.* Above and beyond the bonds of schooling and earth.

On the flip side of that thought, I know an engineer, a physicist and a fighter pilot who have all asked themselves at one time or another, 'What if?' What if it's possible? Einstein did. Truly great minds think outside of the norm. All the time.

NASA's people, mostly scientists and engineers, are the great explorers of our time, without whose imaginations, we'd still be gazing at the moon saying, "Hmmmm. I wonder if anyone lives there." How fantastic was the idea of outer space travel when they first floated the notion?

Remember the Neurosurgeon whose reasoning about Near Death Experiences was drenched in earthly medical science and easily explainable? Nothing to it! Lack of Oxygen to the brain! A dying brain's imaginings! NDE's? Absolutely absurd! Until, he experienced a Near Death Experience of his own. At which point he knew, and had to say, that there is something else going on, my friends! He was convinced that there is a vibrant consciousness that does not depend on a physical, living brain.

The universe works in strange ways.

It's true that not everybody can make that reach into, and beyond, other dimensions without proof of some kind. And all too often, that truth is difficult to explain or demonstrate. The only way, for most people to believe without doubt, myself included, is through personnel experience. It is only then that we can begin to take a second look at the experiences of others and say, 'Wow!"

That's exactly what Steve Jobs, the computer guru reportedly said right before he transitioned to the Other Side. "Wow!"

...as it is in Heaven

Chapter 26: Danny and Jane

Postman's Knock

"Where are you going?"

That's my mommy dearest. Why does she always have to know everything! 'Where are you going? What are you doing?' It's totally boring! I mean, I'm almost *seventeen*, aren't I? I should be able to go places without being grilled like a salmon on a spit! "To grab a milkshake and fries at the Milky Way." I shout. Here comes the 'who with' . . .

"Who with?"

"I'm driving myself–and going to meet Danny." I knew that would be the next question.

"Oh. Didn't you just break up with him?"

I knew that was coming too, "Yup. But we made up." That's all I'm going to tell her. There's no need for her to know everything that goes on in my life. And no way am I going to tell her that the reason for the break up was that Danny drives like a maniac.

Talk about no boundaries! My mom's the poster child of No Boundaries.

"Well, be careful." Slight hesitation in mom's voice. Like she wants to know more, then, "Don't be too long."

She's such a nervous ninny! Like I said, I'm sixteen and nine tenths, already. She freaks out about everything and says I will too one day when my kid starts driving. She is sooo totally wrong. I will *never* treat my kids like this. "Okay. Can I take your car? It's behind mine in the driveway."

"Yes. Be careful!"

"Okay." See what I mean?

"Don't roll your eyes at me, young woman."

"Okay," Yay, I get to drive her Audi! Not that it's that cute or anything, in fact it's kind of old lady-ish, but I like the feel of it. I like it a lot better than her ten year old Toyota that I'm usually expected to drive.

I run down the short driveway to where her car is parked and have my hand on the door when I hear her call. Now what?

"Janey, wait! I forgot to mail this. Will you run by the Post Office, please?"

"Sure!" I run back up the driveway and snatch the letter out of her hand, anxious to be gone. I told Danny I'd pick him up at his house, which is almost on the way to the village, but not quite. In fact it's about five miles off the main road on a steep, narrow road that climbs up the side of the mountain. That too, was omitted in my inquisition with Mommy Dearest. Citing the Need to Know basis.

I place the envelope on the dash and back out of the driveway. Very carefully, because I know full well she's watching me like a hawk. That's the trouble–it's like living in fish bowl around here. I'm under constant surveillance.

The tires crunch over the stones on Danny's driveway as I drive up to the front of his house. He's standing on his porch, texting or something, but when I draw up level with the steps, he comes bounding down with his hands in his jeans pockets.

"Cool! How'd you get your mom's car?" He runs his hand over the hood. "Can I drive?"

"Maybe. On the way back." I lie. Really? He must think I'm crazy! I just said that to make him feel good. There's no way he's going to drive back. My mom and dad's reach, as in telescopic eyes and such, is phenomenal. It would be just my luck to let him drive and run into my dad on his way home from work. Either that or one of the blue-haired lady bridge friends would see us, and the next thing you know, mom would be on the phone telling me to get Danny out of the driver's seat. NOW! Plus about a hundred other choice words I don't feel like hearing.

It's mid-afternoon when we get down into the tiny village of Norton on The River and it's jam-packed with people who've come to watch the fireworks show they put on every July 4th. I see some kids we know riding their bikes up and down the street. Danny waves to a group of them on the sidewalk outside the Apollo movie theater.

Marsha Baker's standing there with the group of mostly guys, flirting as usual. She gives Danny a kind of slow-moving, sweeping eye lash look that just screams *'Hi Cutie!'* And he falls for it every time, adjusting his seat, to reflect Mr. Cool, as he straightens up and casually, so casually, runs a hand through his hair, never taking his eyes off her. I wish

I had an ejection button on his seat. But, on the other hand, who can blame him? She's movie star gorgeous and I wish I was her . . . and then I think, No, I don't! And poke Danny in the ribs instead. Hard.

"Hey! What'd you do that for?" He blurts out rubbing his side.

I just give him one of those slow-moving Marsha looks and pull into a parking space. No comment.

The Milky Way Ice Cream parlor is only a block away so we get out of the car and walk. There are a ton of kids we don't know mostly sitting at the outside cafés talking on their phones or walking along the waterfront. It's a warm and breezy afternoon and spray from the fountain in the square blows all over us as we pass.

We go inside and sit down at a booth beside the window. "Where do all these guys come from?" Danny looks around to see who's new and if there's anyone he knows. "We don't know half of them!"

"Hi Janey!" A girl calls from a nearby booth.

That's Debbie Reynolds. Her folks named her after some old movie star. Can you believe it? I'd die if my folks had done that. "Hi, Deb," I answer, stringing my purse over the back of my seat.

Danny puts two mountainous glasses of fluffy ice cream down in front of us. I don't want to talk to Debbie Reynolds so I lower my head and take a slurp out of my straw looking around on the QT to see who else is there. No one I know, so I concentrate on the cherry cream concoction in front of me, raising my head as some loony tunes comes wheeling in on a skate board. So un-cool.

"Damn! Did you see that? That dork nearly ran over those girls!" Danny chuckles raising his glass to his lips and slurping up the dregs of his Sundae.

"So, tell me again why I had to pick you up–instead of the other, way around," I say, watching the skate board guy bump a waitress carrying a tray of milk shakes. She holds on tight, shouting *'IDIOT!'* as he passes.

Danny leans back against the blue vinyl seat with his hands clasped behind his head. "I got into trouble for borrowing my dad's car without asking last week."

"Hmmm."

". . . and smashed up the bumper. And a tail light."

"How'd that happen?"

"I backed into a dump truck leaving a parking lot."

"Was your dad mad?"

"Huh! Mad's not the word for it! He yelled for about an hour about not paying attention, said something about being 'haphazard and mindless, and that's what comes from being sneaky—and an irresponsible and inexperienced driver.' And if he had his way, no one would be turned loose in a car until they were 30! Blah, blah, blah, and then he grounded me from driving for a month. How'm I supposed to get experience if I'm grounded from driving, I'd like to know?"

I shrug and cast him a sidelong glance. He really is an idiot. I mean, he's driving without permission and *backs into a dump truck?* Are you kidding me?

As we're walking out, Danny holds out his hand for the keys.

"Are you crazy?" I say. "You just told me you banged up your dad's car. Now you want the keys?"

"Aw, come on, Janey!" He begs, looking around to see who's watching. "Please?"

269

My phone rings just at the right moment, thank goodness, because this is getting to be AWK-WARD! "It's my mom, I need to call her back, let's go!" Opening the driver's side door I plop myself down as he walks huffily around to the other side of the car. I mean–does he really think I would let a proven and convicted bad driver near my mom's car! Seriously.

I call my house and Mom asks when am I coming home, and don't forget the letter. And that's a good thing because I'd already forgotten it.

We drive slowly out of the village with Danny muttering and staring out of the window, and begin the climb back up the mountain. I open the sun roof and let the air stream through the car, turn the radio up and slide down the windows.

"Wheeeeee!" I yell. "How great is this! Feel how cool the air is!" My hair swirls around my head, lifted by the wind blowing down from the hills and through the car windows. I feel young and free and sassy. So I put my foot down and the Audi gathers speed as we crest the first hill and begin the roll down the other side. The trees are bright summer green and the sunlight shining through their leaves dapples the blacktop like lace as it disappears under the tires.

We roll down the steep hill, into the dip, and into the shadowy valley with giant oaks on either side of the road that hide the sun, leaving the mossy rocks in dark shadow as we climb the next hill. Up, up we go, into the sunshine, taking the curves wide and spinning into the next one on the S-bends.

"Steady," I hear Danny say. "Slow it down!" he says as he raises both his arms through the sunroof and throws his head back on the headrest.

On the radio Mariah Carey is belting out her latest and we sing along with Danny drumming his fingers on the dash and I'm tapping my fingers on the steering wheel, keeping time with the music as the car crests the next hill, takes the steep curve and begins to gather speed on the downhill slope.

I fling my arm out of the window, feeling the adrenalin rush through my veins and I yell "Wheeeee!" The sunlight is blinding now that we're out of the valley, right at eye-level as the great white globe starts its slow descent into dusk. But that's not going to happen for another hour, probably, and right now it is streaming into my eyes making me squint and lower the sun visor. Just at that moment, a missile skids out of the blue and hits my cheek bone under my eye.

271

"OW!" My eye is watering and I hit the brakes, swiping the back of my hand across my eye and staring at the object in my lap. It's my mom's letter.

Danny lurches forward, barely managing to brace himself before the dash comes up to hit his head. "Look out!" he shouts. "Watch the road! What are you doing?" He's rubbing his head where the dash has left a mark.

"Sorry! The letter flew off the dash and hit me in the face. The corner nicked my eye. . . Oh *No*! I forgot to mail the letter! Hold on, I'm turning around–we've got to go back to town!"

"Jeese! Slow down Janey! You're going too fast–watch where you're going! Slow down, or let me drive!"

"Okay, right after this curve when we get to the bottom of the hill. I LOVE this car!" I start to laugh but then I see the look on his face and my giddiness dies in mid stream. He looks so funny! He's staring at the rear view mirror. "What is it?" yell.

"Oh, SHIT! Look what's coming at us!" Danny shouts.

Checking the side mirror, I see that there's an eighteen wheeler barreling down behind us with its horn blasting, brakes screeching, and it's gaining on us–fast. Oh, my God! "It's out of control!" I shout. All I can see is the giant blue cab bearing down on us. I don't know whether to scream or hold up my hands and cover my face and wait to die.

Then Danny's voice breaks through the panic. "He's got no brakes! Pull over!" He yells. "Pull over NOW!"

"*I can't!* There's nowhere . . ."

"Find a place! Jesus! He's going to run us down! We're dead!"

Danny's face is as white as a ghost. I'll never forget it. "Get over, Janey! Move over! *Now!*"

The truck is almost on top of us and I can see the driver gesticulating wildly. He's got his head out of the window screaming at us.

I scream, the car swerves as I pull over as far as I can, rumbling over stones and high grass and I scream again. "Oh my God! We're going to die!"

"Look!" Danny yells, "right in front of us! Pull in! Pull in!" His left hand grabs for the steering wheel. I scream again and just before I cover my face with both hands, I noticed there's a clearing in front of us, coming up fast. I feel the car tilt and rattle over the roadside shrubbery, tall grass scraping its side, dirt flying up in a cloud of red dust, raining pebbles onto the hood.

Behind us I can hear the scream of tall steel rims on asphalt and smell burning rubber as the huge truck careens downhill with no brakes. A whoosh of hot air lifts my hair as he speeds past us, inches off the Audi's back bumper, rocking the car, and I scream.

Danny's almost on my side of the car, both hands on the steering wheel, trying to steady its course. "*Brake, Jane! Brake!*"

Somehow, I manage to find the pedal and slam it into the floor before we hit a low stone wall that's been put there to stop drivers like me from spinning over the edge of the mountain. The jarring brake flings me up against the steering wheel and I hear Danny groan as the car bumps and spins along the edge of an asphalt parking lot.

Seizing the wheel from Danny, who has been thrown back against the passenger seat, I swing the car into the clearing stopping crazily in front of a giant flag pole and a small red brick post office.

"Shit!" I hear.

"Are you okay?" My voice quivers as I turn to look at him. I thank God he's still alive and turn my eyes back to the scene in front of us. I sit there staring at the flag pole in the middle of the parking lot–and the American flag flapping in the breeze right above the sign clearly marked, US POST OFFICE.

We must be on the wrong road. There isn't a post office on this road . . . I begin to cry. Danny puts his head down in his hands and all we can hear is the screeching of gears, and the tearing of steel as the giant truck comes to a grinding stop at the bottom of the hill. The sound seems to go on and on forever. Until it stops, and the big steel hulk lets out a final groan as its bumper sinks into the stony earth of the hillside.

It feels like time has stopped. The radio's still playing inside the car and Faith Hill is singing "Breathe".

"C'mon! Let's go!" The air is full of the stink of hot rubber and black smoke as we heave ourselves out of the car. Danny is running towards the road and down to where the truck lies, jack-knifed across the curve. I follow him and I can see the truck's front wheels jammed into the earth and the driver pulling himself out of his open window and dropping to the ground.

The man looks at his hands for a moment, runs them through his hair and looks back up the hill at us running towards him. "You kids okay?" He shouts.

My legs are shaking so bad I have to stop and lean against a mile marker on the side of the road. If my face is as pale as I feel, it must be as white as ash. I feel like a piece of white asparagus; limp and half dead.

Danny turns around and tells me to sit down, back off the side of the road. So I do. I see the truck driver's standing with his hands on his hips as Danny reaches him.

"We're good," he tells the driver. "How about you? You okay? Your truck's a mess!"

"Lost my brakes," the man's saying as he runs a hand over his forearm that's badly cut and bleeding.

I get up gingerly and walk over to where they're standing. "You're bleeding."

"Looks worse than it is," he shrugs. "I'll get it 'tended to later."

"I didn't know what to do. There's nowhere to pull off on this road," I say "But then we saw the post office in the clearing and I pulled onto the driveway. I don't know what would have happened if it hadn't been there . . ." My voice fades as I see the look on the truck driver's face.

"What Post Office?" He asks.

I wave my arm towards the Audi up the hill.

"There's no Post Office there," he shades his eyes against the sun and scans the roadside.

Danny and I both turn around. We're staring at the place where the car is sitting on a rough widening of the road surrounded by bushes and tall trees, scratched and dusty but in one piece. There is no flagpole there. And the small, red brick post office is gone. There's nothing but rocky shale, dirt and broken bushes . . .

"What the . . . ? Where's the Post Office?" Danny's staring at the place where we roared off the road and looks around wildly. "I saw it! I swear to God there was a Post Office!"

I look around stunned. It was nowhere to be seen. No flag, no pole, no post office. And no stone wall! It's vanished too! All that's there is a rough pull off on the very edge of a steep embankment, with my mom's car standing in the middle of it.

The trucker removes his cap and rubs a hand over his head. "Well, I don' know what you kids saw, but I ain't never seen no Post Office on this road."

Me neither. I feel as though I'm going to be sick. I know how bad this could have been, and the numbness from the scare is wearing wear off, but a surreal glimpse at something unreal has taken its place and it's making me think I'm going to faint any moment now.

"Can you guys give me a ride back to town?" The man asks. "I need to find a wrecker–and a new phone. "Look at this." He holds up his mangled phone.

"Sure," Danny said. "And we need a post office," he adds quietly as we walk silently up the hill to the car.

The driver looks at him, "You sure you okay? Might not be a bad idee to get you and the girl checked out at the clinic down main street. Y'all could bin knocked in the head or somethin'." He has wrapped a grubby looking hand towel around his arm and I see that blood is beginning to seep through it as he holds it against his side.

Now I know I'm going to lose it. I gag and race for the edge of the clearing, put my hands on my knees and up-chuck my darn cherry ice cream all over the rocks on the embankment. On any other day this would have been sooo uncool . . . I wait a moment, catching my breath, then slowly stand up, wipe a hand across my mouth and stare at Danny and the truck driver who are staring at me like they'd never seen anyone throw up before. And then I look behind them. There is still no post office and no flag. I don't know what I expected.

My legs are wobbly, still unsteady as I walk towards them. In fact all of me is trembling and I feel pale again. And idiotic. "Please will you drive, Danny?" I say in a small voice.

"Sure," he puts an arm around my shoulders, opens the passenger door for me and gestures to the truck driver to get into the car. "Let's go, you need to get that arm looked at," he tells him.

"You did great," he says to me, buckling his seat belt. "You got off the road just in time and that's what saved our lives."

I smiled weakly. He can be really nice sometimes. I shook my head "I wasn't the one who saved our lives; I nearly killed us. But *something* did!"

~

What just happened? How did it just happen that there was a Post Office on the side of the road at the exact time they had to pull over or be killed by a runaway truck? How did a Post Office that had never been there before just suddenly appear? It was there one minute–both the boy and the girl saw it–and gone the next. And why a Post Office? Was it because it was on their minds, and sure to get their attention with the big red, white and blue flag waving them in?

Or was there a deeper message in the vision of the small, red brick building? A Post Office is a place to send and receive messages. I think that the message was received.

Do you believe in Angels?

Chapter 27: Christopher John

"My heart knows where to find you . . ."

I was fourteen when I changed my name to C.J. I mean, seriously? Who wouldn't? The announcement made my mom sigh and shake her head and my dad just stared at me over the black rims of his reading glasses and went back to reading the paper. I kept trying to tell them I was going to do it but no one was listening, apparently.

I mean, have you any idea what it's like to haul a double-barreled name around with you when you're a kid? To start with, no one can remember it and it always gets shortened to Chris or John–athletic instructors prefer to use 'Buddy' or 'Hey, you!' And sometimes, 'Kid!

So, I changed my name, by personal acclamation, from Christopher John to CJ the day after I joined the boy-band in my neighborhood. No dots in between the C and the J– just CJ

~

The name change thing came to a head one late summer day, on the banks of the Mississippi, beside a shallow cove where everyone and his dog was swimming. I was something of a loner, too shy to join them so I sat by myself on an old withered tree stump up the beach a ways and strummed my guitar while people ate their hamburgers.

That guitar went everywhere with me. I liked The Everley Brothers, so I played "Wake up Little Suzie" and then "Cotton Fields," and the prison ballad "Tom Dooley". I didn't notice that they had all turned their heads and were listening; my eyes were fixed on the movement of my fingers and all I heard was the music. In fact, I didn't lift my head until I struck the last few notes, hit the base keys and sang deeply, *"Hang down your head, Tom Dooley–po' boy you're bound to. . . die!"*

The place exploded! Well, that might be an exaggeration–but it definitely popped. Somebody whistled, someone shouted "YEAH!" and the girls clapped and shouted my name. Wow! They were cheering for me! I could feel the familiar wave of red heat creep up my neck and light up my face. Dang! If my hair caught fire any moment now, I wouldn't be surprised. My cheeks were sure burnin' up! So, to cover up my pleasure, I played another tune. This time it was Brenda Lee's "Let's Jump the Broomstick," and some of the girls started to dance in the sand.

And when someone yelled, *"Elvis*! Play Elvis!"

I picked up the refrain of the heart throb of the day's "Teddy Bear" and the girl's went wild.

Well, the very next day, the boy band leader came looking for me and asked if I wanted to play with them next Saturday night at a party at someone's house. Are you kidding me! I prob'ly wouldn't sleep a wink for the next five days!

And on the Monday after the hop, they invited me to be a part of the band and that's when the drummer decided I should change my name To be exact, my wise ass friend, the fifteen year old drummer, told me that I *had* to change my name or people were going to think I was a weirdo. "Trust me, Dude," he said, "There are NO famous guitar players named Christopher John."

I needed no convincing. For two years I had quietly longed to be a part of the band and there was no way I was going to screw this up, so I had no problem becoming

"CJ" Cristopher John went to bed that night and woke up in the brand new world of CJ

The days of sitting on the sidelines, listening to them tune up their instruments and wishing I could join them were over. They were gone, by golly! The nights of solitary strumming in the basement, teaching myself the chords and imitating the sounds I heard from my stack of recordings of everyone from Bill Haley to Elvis, were Over. Done with a capital 'D'! I never thought it would happen. But it had.

~

I really liked my new name. CJ. It made me want to clench my jaw like John Wayne and pull my shoulders back when one of the girls waved her pinky finger at me in the gym one day. It made me grin when one of the seniors yelled, "Hey, CJ!" and smacked me on the back in the hallway at school, almost making me dive head first into the linoleum. Holy shit! I thought I'd lost my balance but I hadn't. Just straightened up, and as cool as you please, I sucked in my breath and managed a "Hey, man!"

So CJ it was. Member of the band, Green Springs Junior Hi School ambassador to the Nashville scene, The Louisiana Hay Ride, Ed Sullivan Show and neon lights! And all that vicarious horse shit fame, made me glow.

~

I lived as CJ for about two years, before reconsidering at the age of sixteen, when, after a trip to the Rocky Mountains with my folks, (who still called me Christopher John), I changed my professional name again, to "Colorado Cool". What a name! It carried the echoes of the canyons, the might of the Rockies, the cool, green waters of thrashing rivers. What a name!

The boy-band changed over the years as they always do. Members graduated and moved onto jobs, or moved away to college, and when I was seventeen, I moved into the role of lead singer and man oh man! I was *loving* it! We played at all the high school dances now, some of the prom parties, and Holy shit! We even landed a gig at the Mississippi State Fair one year.

Girls, I noticed, not to be bragging or anything, liked me. I could have dated plenty, if I'd had the time. I tried it a couple of times, once with a girl I really liked. A real sweetheart. And totally messed the whole thing up. As the little sweetheart told me, "You're no fun to go to dances with. You don't stay off the stage long enough to dance with me!"

Needless to say, that budding romance was in the tank.

Playing in the band had drawbacks. I didn't know the first thing about how to be a date. The next time I got up the nerve to ask a girl to go out with me was when we were trying out another singer, and I thought I had the night off. But, as luck would have it, the new guy didn't show, and this second date of mine ended badly too when lone wolf Fred Minton came onto her, moved in, and danced with her all the time I was on stage and even when I wasn't.

The next day at school, the lovebirds could be seen coochie-cooing all over the campus and that was the end of that. My dad said, "Don't worry about it! Your time will come."

In his dreams! Frankly, I couldn't see it happening, so I just kept on singing and strumming with the band resigning myself to never having another date.

But my life was full. I was writing some of my own songs now, but still playing the hits they grooved to. And then a few months later, I soon forgot about being a total flop when it came to girls because things came almost full circle when several band members graduated, and those of us that were left, re-formed and created a new band. I took the lead role, ditched the name Colorado Cool, and began calling myself and our newly-founded group, "C.J. Parry."(That would be, C dot J dot although everyone still called me CJ) And so it was. The name had just enough cool, just enough swagger and a dash of Nashville swing. And it didn't take long to catch on. The C.J. Parry Band ruled on campus and we were in demand at events all around the county.

And all of that was important; *very* important, because in my senior year, I fell in love with Missy Perkins. In fact, looking back on it, I think I'd been in love with Missy since I was born. I couldn't remember much about how it had evolved—or being born, for that matter. All I knew was that I had loved her as far back as I could remember. Which was about fifteen years. To be precise, it began the year we both started Pre-school.

I remember it well. Standing all alone on that first day of school, scared stiff of the newness, including my new sneakers with laces, not sure whether I would remember how to tie them or not. I missed my mom as soon as she left. But then the gate opened and a pretty lady walked in holding Missy Perkins by the hand, leading her into the throng of children who were gathered around the person they said was to be our teacher. The former me, Christopher John, had never seen anything as perfect as Missy Perkins. I never thought she was an angel or anything like that. The angel on my Christmas tree had squinty eyes and a yellow dress that was unraveling in the back and Missy was nothing like that. Still, she could be an angel, I supposed. She definitely wasn't the kind that cropped up in Sunday school class. She was much prettier. I guess I knew deep down, that she probably wasn't a bona fide Angel, but she was the closest thing to one I'd ever seen. What else could a rosy-cheeked, golden haired little girl with green eyes be?

All that thinking changed quite quickly 'though when she stuck her tongue out at me on the playground when I tried to talk to her, I knew for sure then that Missy Perkins wasn't a real Angel. But I didn't care. In fact it just made me love her even more.

This one-sided love of mine went on well into Middle School even though the queen of my heart didn't seem to know I was alive. But it didn't matter.

Then came the day when I became something of a football hero.

It was an orange-red fall day, and the seventh grade football team was playing its first home game. Missy was standing on the sidelines of the football field in a pale blue short skirt, waving blue and white pompoms and jumping up and down cheering with a band of cheerleaders. Just the sight of her made me take a deep breath and go storming out onto the field, practically snorting like a bull with the rest of the team.

The girls cheered all game long and sometimes they cheered at the right times and sometimes they didn't but the former Christopher John didn't care; especially when I picked up the ball and ran it all the way down the field to score. That was right before I got run over, and trampled into the ground by the entire visiting team.

If memory serves me, I think she was cheering for me as I picked myself up out of the dirt and wiped my bleeding nose on my sleeve. All I could hear was my name, "CJ! CJ!" coming off her sweet lips.

I grinned at her, all beat up and bruised, bloody and dirt-trodden! That was the day I knew without any doubt I could do anything! And I *would* do anything for Missy Perkins 'til the day I died.

We went whooping off the field and even though she practically ignored me for most of the rest of that year, I never forgot that day

Then came the day, that glorious day, when, Missy Perkins came running out of the lake, on the edge of town, where everyone went to swim during the long, hot summers of Green Springs, and there and then, under the big 'ol Live Oak, she bounced to a stop right in front of me. I couldn't breathe so there wasn't any point in trying to say something to this Barbie doll with her halo of cotton blonde hair, standing there just smilin' up at me, so I just blinked. And then, just as sweet as you please, hands on her hips, head cocked to one side, she said, "CJ Parry, I'm having a party, wanna come? It's my sixteenth birthday party!"

I still couldn't breathe but there were three or four of her girl friends standing over to one side giggling, which made me think I better start breathing, and say something or they were liable to swarm. Sure! Was the only thing that came to mind so I said, "Sure!"

And with that she smiled big and swung away from me holding up five fingers, headed to where her friends were and shouted over her shoulder, "Saturday at five at my place!"

CJ Cool managed to hold up one thumb in answer, thinking his grin was about to swallow him whole. Saturday at five! You bet your sweet li'l heart I'll be there!

That was another day I never forgot. Or the way she looked standing there in her flowery shoe-string bikini, and sun burned cheeks, balancing on long tanned legs that reached into a part of him that made his head spin and his heart race.

Looking back on it I wonder if that's what a near death experience must feel like. Just standing there like a dorky Giant Blue Heron trying to keep my heart from jumping out of my chest like a fool cat fish. And then saying something brilliant like "Sure!" Just that. No ifs, ands or buts, I'd be there! *'Though hell should bar the way!'* as The Highwayman would say. Come hell or high water, my dad would say.

~

Two days after her party, right before the last class of the day, she met me near the lockers at school, separated herself from the three other girls she was walking with, and told me how much she liked chocolate shakes.

So what else was a Mississippi boy supposed to do? I bought her a milk shake after school. Damn straight! Three days after that I took her to the movies.

The next week, one of the ever-present girlfriends grabbed my arm in the hallway at school in a bird claw grip and whispered in my ear, "Missy thinks you're cute!"

That's when I dropped my books and my heart started that chicken-scratch jig again. And damn near stopped when the girl of my dreams bent down beside me, smiled softly and began to help me pick them up. My mind must have temporarily left the building because all I can remember was the smell of strawberries in her hair.

What can I say? It confused the hell out of me. CJ Cool? Not anymore. But inside this mass of confusion and unplugged wires, I was beginning to kinda like this outta body feeling I got whenever I saw her. So, when the weekend came I invited her to go on a picnic with me at the lake.

~

She was waiting for me, sitting on the porch swing, swinging her legs, all peachy golden and tanned in white shorts and a red polka dot top. She jumped up as I got out of my car and flicked a bug off the newly polished candy apple red hood, and opened the door as she came bouncing down the steps towards me.

The day was Mississippi hot and there were tiny dots of perspiration speckling her upper lip above that rose- colored mouth of hers. Which was nothing compared to the fact that I was sweating bullets as I reached through the window at the DQ and took two hamburgers and two chocolate shakes from the girl in the window.

I would not spill this stuff. For once, my heart was finally in charge and acting like it should. "I got this," I told her, and carefully set the 'burgers on the front seat and handed a milk shake to Missy. I watched as she bent her head to the straw and sipped. Lord have mercy! I could feel the flush starting somewhere in my chest and climbing into my neck and face. And it had nothing to do with the climate in the marshy Delta.

The asphalt was shimmering as we drove the three mile stretch to the beach. The sun was blinding, sparking off the cars in the sandy parking lot as we left the truck and walked down to the lakeshore. A crowd of kids were sitting on brightly colored towels and mats under the sprawling Live Oak tree that had been there all my life.

I spread Missy's straw mat on the sand and stretched my towel out beside it, waved to some kids we knew and heard Missy call out to some girls in the water.

With the bag of burgers and shakes on the sand between us, Missy sat down beside me under the big tree and tied her hair back with a white ribbon. I handed her a 'burger, and for a moment I could swear her hand touched mine.

Heart trouble again . . . I prayed she wouldn't hear it hammering through my rib cage and the Ricky Valance tee-shirt I had on.

~

Two weeks later, I kissed her for the first time, beside the lake, in the middle of a crowd of people cooking hot dogs. She gave a little gasp. I don't know what made me do it— maybe it had something to do with the glow in her cheeks on that summer evening, or the ketchup smear on her upper lip. Who knew, and I didn't waste any time thinking about it as I kissed her again and this time she kissed me back.

~

It was sometime near the end of the summer of our junior year, I can't remember exactly when, that we went down to the lake alone and swam naked under what should have been a full moon. We never saw the moon, and we never noticed it was missing. Here at the lake the skies had clouded over early in the evening, and the moonlight was shrouded by a cloak of mist and dark gray clouds.

We never noticed that either. The feel of her bare skin under my hands was all I could think of and the shy touch

294

of her fingers on my chest and on my neck, took me away as I pulled her close to me in the cool, wind-brushed water.

As the first heavy drops fell we swam to shore and scrambled out of the water for the shelter of the Oak grove where the tree's massive boughs swept the sand. The air was warm but a sharp breeze had started to ripple the water and pretty soon, large rain drops were plinking off the leaves, speckling the sand as they came down hard.

Thunder rumbled through the pine forests miles away from where we were, and heat lightning danced on the horizon searing the sky, silvering the tops of massive clouds.

A full moon would have been nice but I couldn't worry about that right now. Her skin felt like silk under my hands, the rain drops peppered my bare shoulders, and the summer breeze made me hold her closer. The lyrics to a new song were rising up inside me as I held Missy Perkins in the sand, in the rain. I knew that there would be a rainbow in that song, but for now it could wait.

~

The senior year flew by like a live Nascar race at full tilt. School work, tests, college applications, football, movie and popcorn dates with Missy tumbled over each other for priority. Now, at the end of May, school was nearly over.

There was a post-graduation party at Missy's church tomorrow and it was all the girls could talk about. They had spent the whole day together decorating the hall with streamers and stars and paper lanterns. And tonight, which also happened to be Missy's eighteenth birthday, a group from the senior class were getting together to cook out at one of the girl's houses way on the other side of town.

It was an exciting time, and I was more excited than anyone because the surprise I had planned for Missy's birthday her would blow her away! She was going to Love it! In fact, I was more excited about the surprise than anything else that was going on.

So, with my hair combed back and still damp from the shower, I took the stairs, two at a time, yelled "Bye" to the dog who was snoozing in the yard, and ran out to the car.

Laying my guitar down flat on the back seat, I slammed the door and jumped in behind the wheel. I could hardly wait to see Missy. She was probably at the girlfriend's house by now.

The bulge in my shirt pocket told me I still had her present. It had taken weeks to get it just right and as soon as I got the words and the music running together like soft ice cream, I'd charged off to the recording studio down town, and recorded the song I'd written her for her birthday.

That was yesterday. Once again I patted my pocket, feeling the outline of the cassette. I'd find the right time to give it to her later that evening, but for now, all I could think of was her face when I began to sing for her. Composed, written, produced and sung by, listen to this, Ladies and Gentlemen, CJ Parry, Lead singer of *the* C.J. Parry Band!

I was grinning so hard, my jaw ached. But it was good! The song was good! It was about young love, the end of High School and the separation looming in September when we both went far away from Green Springs, Mississippi to begin the next phase of our lives. The song captured the mood, the lyric captured the emotions of loving and leaving, and the music carried it into whatever the future might bring. It was sad and exciting all rolled in one and it was worth all the midnight hours it took to get it right.

'To begin the next phase of our lives,' I thought again. Missy was bound for college in Pennsylvania, and I was headed to naval boot camp in San Diego. Anchors Away and all that good shit!

~

The party was hopping when I got there. I found Missy and lost her again as she ran off with her trio of girls to help carry the trays of cup cakes and fruit punch onto the porch.

I joined the boys from the band who were sitting on a low stone wall on the patio and lay my guitar on an unused table. We weren't playing tonight we were all just there to have fun. This was our party. The Graduates! The Class of '61 and the hot shots on campus! And this was our last night together. Or it might be. Who knew where we'd all wind up or if we'd ever be together like this again?

It was a scary thought. The draft was in full swing as the Indo-Chinese war heated up and there were rumors of the imminent deployment of American troops, maybe as early as the fall. A shiver skittered between my shoulder blades and I couldn't tell whether it was some sort of weird excitement or fear. But I guessed it could be both.

Three or four of us had already signed up, while a few others were college bound, and I heard one kid say he had a job rough necking in the oil fields of Texas. The military had turned him down for some medical reason or other.

They had a victrola playing 45's in the corner and some of the girls got up to dance. The night wore on, people talked about tomorrow and beyond tomorrow, they talked about graduation and the kids who'd made it, and the kids who hadn't. Mickey Ortez, talked about Mississippi State and the football scholarship they'd given him, and then darn near broke his neck doing a crazy limbo.

Burgers sizzled on the grill, marshmallows burned black on the end of sharpened sticks, and everybody danced. Well, except for Joey Cameron who led some of the guys out back for a smoke and a Dixie cup of the local 'shine.

I ate a burger, then another one, they cut the birthday cake with Missy's name scrawled across the top, and everyone sang "Happy Birthday". I hugged my girl, and when there was a lull in the chatter I held my guitar up and said, "Can I play something? Got something I want to play for Missy's birthday."

"If music be the food of *luuuvv*," one of the girls trilled dramatically, standing with a hand on her heart, the other arm outstretched, gazing dreamily up at the sky intoning from the Shakespeare play we'd just finished reading.

"Shut up, Izzy!" Someone giggled.

"Play on! Give me excess of it!" yelled one of the band members, finishing the quote with a swagger and cracking up the group.

"Shut up, dorks!" C.J. Parry's drummer yelled. "Play, CJ–let's hear it."

I grinned, and settled myself down on a stool. "Missy, this is for you." I looked for her and patted the concrete bench beside me. "Come sit by me." I waited as she shyly took a seat.

"It's called, 'Missy's Song'. I know! Very creative!" I snorted self-consciously, "but that's what it's called." And I hit the first chord. I smiled at Missy and she smiled back.

"Where will we go, from here, Missy? What winding paths will we follow?

Will there be music, excitement and fear in my dreams of a new tomorrow?

Dark clouds hide the moon and her light from view blurring the road ahead,

300

The lightning strikes, the music stops and my heart is filled with dread.

As the canons roar, and the earth explodes pulling us apart, I never forget you're here in my soul, forever in my heart.

When the fighting is done, when the battle cries die and the music plays again

We'll be together forever my love beyond the tears and pain.

Music will fill the air again, as moonlight plays on the shore,

I'll hold you near, there'll be no fear when the thunder starts to roar.

When the clouds hide the light of the moon from me, I'll find my way back home,

For you are my light, that voice in the night, that's guided me all along.

My heart knows where to find you, my love will find its way,

Through ice and snow and lightning strikes—'though hell should bar the way!

You're only a heartbeat away from me until we are together

I'll find you on that rainbow shore, you'll be in my arms forever."

My fingers trailed on the last note of the song and I raised my eyes to meet hers.

Missy's eyes were wet, her hands clasped together across her breast. I was pretty sure she liked it. The words were sweet–and sad–that's why she cried . . . but it felt like forever before she leaned towards me and hugged me hard. "That was beautiful," she whispered.

I dug into my top pocket and handed her the cassette. "It still is! Don't lose it," I grinned, trying to cover up the briefest moment of shyness.

Missy took my gift and shook her head. "Never."

~

Remember that first love. Remember how alive we felt, how every color seemed brighter, every summer sky was bluer, and the rain on your face on a warm afternoon had never felt so soft? What's more, there seemed to be song birds everywhere, magic filled the moonlight and every love song belonged to us.

Remember the thrill of catching his eye–across a crowded room . . . and the panic when the phone rang–what will I say! Then on that first meeting, when the words that were

302

dying to be spoken, fell away in the wake of her gaze–too shy, too tongue-tied to come up with even the simplest sound. Or worse, did you say "Huh?" When all you really wanted to say was that you were you were dying of love for him? The joy when you held hands for the first time in a dark and musty smelling old movie house . . .Oh, yes, I remember.

This must be where they get their ideas for Hallmark cards. Almost certainly, young love was the inspiration for Monet, Shelley, Strauss . . . for every fairy tale ever written; even those that never found that happily ever after. Like Romeo and Juliet or the lovers on the Titanic. Does life mimic art? We wonder. Or does art mimic life? Whatever the answer, Love is truly a Many Splendored Thing.

~

It was summertime, two years after graduation, when I came home. The Fourth of July to be exact. Homecoming was everything I'd known it would be. My house, white with black shutters, standing in the middle of a Live Oak grove, was strung with red, white and blue bunting, and the blue and gold United States Navy flag hung beside the Stars and Stripes from a tall flagpole near the front gate.

There was at least one new shed in the back yard. Of course there was. They sprung up like mushrooms to accommodate all of Dad's projects; projects that had sprung up overnight when he retired. And some got finished, and others were on hold. Still others just sat there waiting for inspiration, motivation or a bon fire. Planks of wood were stacked in tidy piles beside the tidy sheds, and behind the garage was the old wood pile, waiting for my ax, I suspected, to change it into firewood.

First there would be the tour of the whole place; the wood piles, the sheds and the vegetable garden. I could tell the invitation was hanging in the air and I would follow him and I would come up with the appropriate comments.

"Gotta keep movin' son!" I'd heard that a lot since dad retired. "Minute you stand still something's gonna get you, and if that don't kill you, the doctor's over yonder at the clinic sure as hell will!"

My mother had stocked the refrigerator with everything she thought I liked. The pantry was crammed with Froot Loops and moon pies. Really? Didn't she know how old I was?

"Well, you always used to love them. I wasn't sure whether they had them in the Navy or not."

And I would hug her, and eat a bowl of the brightly colored, sickly sweet cereal rings. Strange thing was, they still tasted pretty darn good.

The family would start arriving in droves. They would all be there, starting at noon, and that evening when all the family hugs and proud parenting simmered down, after all the photographs of new babies and weddings I had missed were passed around, I was able to pry myself away.

You see, there was a party that night down by the lake on the lake in Green Springs, so with promises of, "I won't be late! But don't y'all wait up!" I sprinted down the driveway and jumped behind the wheel of my old Chevy truck, with only one thing on my mind. Missy was waiting for me.

~

The evening was marshy hot, just the way I remembered these hot summer evenings. This Mississippi boy had gotten used to those California summers and this Delta soup bowl was the one thing I could do without. The sun still hung too high above the horizon at seven O'clock, and clouds of gnats still swarmed around the truck as the old engine sprang into life. My guitar was thrown on the back seat, just in case some of the guys from the band showed up for some jammin'. I knew at least one of them wouldn't be there. Jimmy Maples, a first year rookie recruit in the United States Marine Corps, stepped on a landmine on his first tour of active duty overseas in South East Asia and came home in a black bag. It was hell; so was every other senseless part of the Vietnam War.

I shoved the thought aside, and cranked up the AC. The heat of the old home town was climbing all over me. Good thing I had my swim trunks on, because the first chance I got, I was going to race into the water to cool off.

The sandy track to the beach hadn't changed any in the two years I'd been away. Same old crab holes, mud bug nests everywhere, and bleached-white broken clam shells. Thorny nettles and vines draped the grasses and shrubs alongside that were full of garter snakes we used to catch on those long, hot summer days. I parked in what little shade there was in the Live Oak grove, but even it was warm.

A storm that had been trying to break all evening was grumbling low over the horizon, and the truck's windshield was spotted with fresh bug splats. I could hear the cicadas chirping in the grove so loudly that the distant roll of thunder was a muffled, purple backdrop to their symphony. I slammed the truck door shut and reached inside the open window to grab my guitar and a six pack of Schlitz from the back seat then turned and made my way to the beach.

My eyes scanned the crowd of kids between me and the lake, and then I saw her. Missy was standing up to her knees in the water and waving to me. My heart felt like it was about to bust wide open with joy at the sight of her as she ran to meet me, her eyes sparkling, her hair flying wildly in the wind that was starting to pick up. It was another of those moments; a snapshot in time I knew I would never forget and–those that rode with me in my navy helicopter every time I went up.

I was aware of a group of people standing around the grill and in the water, but I had no idea who they were. I only had eyes for Missy and her smile filled the space between me and them.

I felt the warm thump as she flung herself into my arms for the first time in way too long and I held her for a long time feeling the gritty sand along her arms and on her cheeks. The scent of her hair and the sugar sweet aroma of warm, damp girl filled my senses.

And then she pulled away from me, and with a sparkle in her eyes, said, "You can kiss me, if you want to–"

I lost no time as hoots and hollers and a dozen wolf whistles rose up the from the beach. I kissed her long and hard, feeling the months of missing her falling away as she kissed me back and whispered, "I've thought about you—and this, every day!"

My breath caught in my chest. She had no idea how much my heart echoed her words . . . no idea how I had longed to hear these words, no idea that tonight, I would ask her to marry me.

Finally, we pulled apart and walked slowly into the crowd with our arms around each other's waists. We drew apart as I shook hands and clapped a few of the guys on the shoulders, and chatted with some of the girls who came up to hug me and welcome me home. Missy stayed close beside me, smiling, holding on to my arm.

The hot dogs were salty and juicy, one of the girls had made a strawberry dump cake and someone else was passing around a big tray of Mississippi mud cakes. I dabbed a smear of chocolate icing off Missy's chin and sucked it off my finger. I was in Heaven, I decided. And if this wasn't Heaven, it was all the Heaven I needed.

She told me she thought I'd grown. And then she blushed. "What I meant was—"

I kissed her again and looked up grinning. Should I ask her now?

"You just look–I don't know–taller and broader, maybe?" She giggled. "Maybe it's all those rope walls they made you climb or something?"

I laughed out loud, thinking she was prettier than I'd ever seen her. "Missy–" I began but didn't finish because someone was calling to her from the water. It would have to wait.

Much later, when the sun was just a memory, a line of gold on the horizon, and the clouds were sinking down to the water, grey and bruised, moving billows of air, he and two others began to pick on their guitars. The group gathered in close to the sand pit where the guys had built a log fire, as grey and yellow spirals of wood smoke coiled upwards carrying with the scent of burning wood and marshmallows. Sweet and smoky.

In the darkening sky the thunder rumbled over the strumming of guitars and chatter. The storm was getting closer. A light wind was blowing off the lake and they could see the high clouds scudding across the sky, trailing lacey fingers across the moon, tattooing a dark web across its face. The wind picked up the smoke and blew it inshore towards the trees, sending it weaving among strands of Spanish moss and the waxy green leaves of the Oaks.

"Play the Fight Song!" One of the boys shouted.

"Yeah!" The call was echoed around the circle and a group of girls stood up, joined arms and broke into the decades old football rallying song from Green Springs High. The boys picked up the beat on their guitars and soon everyone joined in–laughing, singing and high kicking, mostly out of tune and out of step, but everyone agreed, the fight song had never been sung so well. The old Alma Mater would probably come next, followed by some fast-strumming rock until everyone got tired and either flopped on the beach or went home.

Suddenly a loud clap of thunder split the air on the opposite side of the lake. A couple of the girls squealed and hugged their arms close to their chests. White caps flecked the water, and cold gusts of wind and spray replaced the warm air that had hung like a pall of damp cotton over the beach all evening. It blew from the east and southward towards the ocean some fifty miles away, rattling the oak leaves as a skinny fork of lighting stuck the beach on the far shore.

The jammers kept jamming and some of them launched into another school song, until one of the girls let out a little shriek. "That's coming closer, ya'll!" As she spoke, several deep rumbles roared across the water, followed by a blast of wind that threw white water over the rocks on the curve of the beach.

Missy scrambled to her feet beside me, casting an eye at the threatening storm. "I wonder if we shouldn't go home?"

"Nah, this'll blow over soon," one of the boys said.

"Well it's getting cold! I'm going to the car to get my sweater," she said.

"Hang on! I'll go with you!" I stood up shaking the sand out of my shorts, watching the water white capping and breaking on some nearby rocks. The trees across the water were waving back and forth and the sand was blowing off the top of the beach, dusting the trees and the cars underneath them.

We should head out, I thought grabbing my guitar, racing to catch up with Missy who was running across the beach towards the trees where her car was parked. I could see the sand flying around her as she ducked her head and put her hands over her face to keep it out of her eyes.

Then shockingly, the sky lit up and a fork of lightning danced across the water, streaking it with silver. I watched it shimmy like a tortured demon before hitting the water close by followed by a crack of thunder almost overhead. The first rain drops pitted the surface of the water and the tree tops began to sway in the wind.

"Wheeee!" A girl in the group yelled. "Here it comes! Run for the shack!"

"Missy!" I yelled. "Wait up!" My guitar was slowing me down. I stumbled up across the sand, bent over, and shielding the instrument from the rain, I ran after my girl.

Behind us, people were shouting, grabbing for shoes and shirts, making a beeline for the grass-roofed shack that stood at the back of the beach. It was the only shelter this far down the shore. The closest solid structure was on the main road two miles from where they were, and I planned to try and make it before this monster struck in earnest.

~

But the clouds closed in fast. They were churning right above tree-top level. I hesitated for only a second before running as hard as I could for Missy and the truck. We were right under these trees, a stand-out beacon . . . I knew. The wind blew hard, shaking their canopies and then the storm broke overhead. Rain burst from the vapor-filled pillows of moisture, spilling onto the lake shore, blurring the horizon.

Another sharp crack of thunder shook the sand and the Live Oaks as lightning whistled down, double-forked and deadly, it tore through the tallest of them.

I lunged for Missy hearing her name die on my lips as she fell against the giant tree, just as the trunk was split apart by the power of its strike.

~

The way the newspapers told it, a party at the lake had gone horribly wrong when a monster thunder storm rolled in. One of the girls, told a reporter, "Most of us were crammed into the shack and I saw CJ racing towards Missy . . . I heard him scream, *"Misseeey!* And then, Oh My God— he fell face down on the sand!"

~

"You jest cain't never tell when one of them big ol' summer storms gonna hit," one of the old men sitting on a bench outside the Winn-Dixie market, told the others.

"Now, that's the truth," one of his friends observed. "An' if you was to aks me, they durn lucky onee one of them young'uns lost they life! Coud'a bin that whole shack full of 'em ifn that lightnin' had hit any closer."

~

One person died, the paper said, struck by a lightning bolt that ripped into the oak grove and sent another to the hospital. A group of about 20 youngsters was lucky to be alive after the grass roof of the shack they were sheltering in caught fire when lightning struck the beach close behind it.

~

One of the old men grunted and then they were silent for a moment, mulling over the tragedy that had paralyzed the small Mississippi town. Then one of them spat some baccy juice out of the corner of his mouth and said, "I heared that big ol' Oak—th' one thas bin there since I cain't remember when—done split in two when that lightnin' hit."

"Un, huh. That tree musta bin ov' a hunn'ed years old, you aks me," his friend said. And then they were quiet again, chewing their tobacco, trying to remember back all those years ago. "Least a hunn'd I'd say."

~

Missy died instantly.

CJ lay in the Jackson Medical Center for four days. His guitar stood in a corner of the room, miraculously untouched by the storm. The EMTs had found it lying three feet away from where the boy had fallen. His left hand was stretched out, reaching for the girl, they said. The ground around them was charred with soot. A third of the old oak lay on its side, its massive limbs reaching skyward, its torn trunk glistening white, in the moonlight long after the storm had passed.

"*. . . only a heartbeat away from me. . .*"

~

CJ lingered in that nether world of unknown consciousness, with one side of his body covered with second and third

315

degree burns. His parents were told to expect the worst. Day after day, after long, long day, with no signs of improvement, hope dwindled and it seemed that the doctor's prognosis was right.

But then, one rainy afternoon, as his heart-broken family made the decision to remove him from life support, CJ opened his eyes and his lips began to move for the first time since the lightning strike.

"Missy . . . hit," he said.

The air was misty outside the hospital window. "It's a miracle," someone whispered as his mother and father, choking back tears of joy, reached for their son. His mother held his bandaged hand to her cheek, stroking his hair. "Oh CJ . . . you're alive!" She wept as his father held her.

"We thought—It's a miracle indeed! My son's going to be alright!" The big man turned towards the window and raised his eyes to Heaven. "Thank God! Thank GOD!" He said his voice thick with tears.

Much later he would remember seeing the rainbow that formed above the trees, outside the hospital window and the words of CJ's song came back to him. *"I'll find you on that rainbow shore, you'll be in my arms forever . . ."*

One day, CJ. One day. But not today, my boy.

~

Could it be that from somewhere deep inside the lightest and strongest vibrations of earthly love and music, a premonition had blossomed under CJ's fingers as he played for Missy on the eve of their hi-school graduation?

What are premonitions? Where do they come from? Is it an unconscious fear of something that *might* happen? We all have those. But this was something so farfetched it barely touched the lives of these teenagers on the night before graduation. Why would it, when their worlds were so full of hope and anticipation?

So what happened on that evening many nights ago when the world was alive and warm and vibrant with the joy of graduation? What wind blew through the strings of CJs guitar, through the lyric of his song, lifting the veil that separates us from that other world? Did it part, for just a moment, to show the future?

~

When all is said and done, we have no earthly explanations for any of this; because the sense of premonition is not of this earth. It comes from out of this world, from a place most of us can't remember easily, and a few of us–those of us who are very young–haven't forgotten.

Why is it that swift memories tease us, skitter across our brains, and touch our human consciousness for mere seconds at a time leaving us confused and adrift in their wake? Gossamer sheer and fleeting, they disappear like dawn into day. They dance briefly on wings of iridescence, and then they're gone. Sometimes they come in the brightness of day, sometimes past mid-night, beyond that darkest hour, breaking through the dark velvet of pre-dawn as we teeter on the edge of waking. And sometimes they come unbidden, when the high and light vibrations of that other world are able to break through the veil–when love is in the air, or when the music plays.

Chapter 28: Eve

"It's a dream–glassy and surreal," she said. "It keeps happening."

It's been a mystery for a long, long time, this dream of mine that occurs again and again. My name is Eve, and from the time I was very young, I've had this weird, but beautiful and surreal, dream I never could explain. It was the same every time, and I remember everything about it. It was, and it still is, so real, so vivid in every way. You know–the light, the smells, the warmth–the children. I used to wonder about it all the time, trying to figure out what it meant. Sometimes, when we were in our teens, I would talk to my best friend Jolie about it, but she couldn't figure it out either.

The strangest thing is that every time it happened I could see it coming. I could actually *feel* it coming. That may be more accurate; I could *feel* it coming. It came on like a migraine or something, you know? And it seemed to have its own aura as it approached. Almost like a ship coming through the mist . . .

319

But there was never any pain involved, or anything like that; no, nothing like that. It arrived gently, slowly emerging from the mist.

Back then, when I was a child, we lived in Brewster County in West Texas. Fire-spittin' hot in the summer, and brittle, snappin' cold in the winter. I still remember the wind blowing off the slopes of the Glass Mountains, freezing pellets of rain water hitting the ground making a slushy mess of the dirt road that lead into town.

It was like that the night I helped Mama carry one of the babies to the clinic in the middle of the night. Mama was crying and fit to be tied, all the way there, saying she didn't think the child was breathing. I don't know where the child's daddy was . . . All I remember was how cold the night was and how cold that baby was. I think it died before we got there, but no one ever told me—all I knew was that they just took it away and told us they'd do the arrangements. Then someone took us back to a small kitchen and gave mama and me a bowl of warm beans. Mama gave me hers.

When we got back to the shack we called home, I could hear the wind whistling through the cracks in the plaster and under the plastic they had put over the windows. The tiny abode felt like it might be lifted clear off the ground and blown to bits.

That's how strong the wind gets in West Texas when it blows of the mountains. Plenty of folks have their places blown clear out from under them on nights like that one. I remember how cold my hands were and I couldn't hardly feel my feet. The bed was like a bag of ice and if it hadn't been for three of us sleeping together, me, Francesca and Anna, every one of us would likely have froze to death.

Seems that was the first time the dream came. Just as quiet and sure as it could be. Darned if it doesn't make me think of something I read in one of those English literature books on one of the days I got to go to school–something about . . . the mist coming in on little cat paws–something like that. That's what it was like. Just as soft and purty as can be.

When it first starts, the air in the dream becomes real still and it has a different kind of light. I think of it as the 'dream light'. And as I watch, it melts into a kind of golden sheen like the color of new corn tassels that grow near the Rio Grande. I went there once with one of Mama's men. The light almost shimmers–I can't for the life of me describe it even after all these years. And if I was to try and explain it to anyone they'd think I was slap crazy, so I just kept my mouth shut. Except Jolie. Jolie always listened to what I had to say, and sometimes she would say, "It's not weird—it's like those glassy mountains that don't never seem quite real—but they are. If you could touch that dream, Eve Marie, you'd know that it's real too."

It was strange how the dream filled the spaces all around me with peace. I couldn't hardly tell where its edges were. I guess maybe there were none. Everything just felt sort of soft and quiet. No sound. And then I would breathe in the most delicate scent gently coming off the waving grasses and warm earth. That dream like to just pick me up, wrap itself around me like silk scarves—or kitten fur. Somehow, it became part of me and I was part of it. I used to think this is what it must feel like to snuggle in the heart of new cotton.

And those golden grasslands were all around me for as far as the eye could see, and the earth— oh, mercy! The earth—it was so soft underneath my feet, nothing like that old cutting shale of Brewster County. It was sort of springy— like walking weightless almost. I just remember how it was so very easy to be in that place—very easy to walk through the grasses. And, oh, Lordy, the perfume. It had something in it that just made me want to let go of the world and just be surrounded in it, and in that peace. Indescribable peace. I felt like I was a part of this golden dream place. So safe.

Soon's that happened I would look around and see that I wasn't alone. There was a little boy with me. He was only about five or six years old–'bout the same age as me– and we were happy being together. Just us. Me and him in the grassy meadows, with the smells and the breezes . . . no trees, no fences, no edges . . . just a field full of swaying grasses all around us; walking together through this golden light–not talking, not saying a word–just walking and holding hands.

Sweet. Like sweet tea in summer. My sweet tea–made like only a Texan can make it. Sweet, icy cold and clinking with clear ice. And forget the powdered sugars and crap. This is the real thing. Cane sugar, sweet and pure! Like we put in that old sugar bowl I have that used to belong to Mama, and her mama before her. Now it's mine. It's the real thing. Solid china and real pretty.

Mama liked pretty things. We were dirt poor–the wrong side of the tracks was too rich for us, so she didn't have much of anything. Nothing nice, anyways. That always made me feel sad when I walked by Bounty Mart store down town and saw all that fancy stuff in the windows, you know, flowery stuff I knew she'd never have. I would stand there staring through the windows sometimes feeling like it had suddenly gotten cold around me–like the sun went behind a cloud.

When I think of Mama from all those years ago, I see her as pretty as she was before life drug her through the dust. People use to say that her granddaddy and my great-granddaddy, was a full-blood Apache. Supposedly he grabbed a young Spanish girl during a raid in one of the border towns one night, packed her on the back of his pony, and galloped hell bent for the mountains of West Texas. That's where I got my love of horses from, I guess and that's prob'ly where Mama got her looks. Her hair, as black as onyx, fell down to her waist, and sometimes it glittered in the sunlight.

Pretty as a picture, she shone like glass in the dusty shale of the oil fields—and drew men to her like honey bees to clover. Mama loved men too, which was a good thing looking back on it, because it was what helped her to survive. But it could be a bad thing too depending on which man happened to be hanging around at the time. Some of them were downright mean, coming out of the oil fields of Pecos County—rowdy, hell-raising towns like Big Lake where the lawmen were hard to find when the brawls broke out. I guess rough-necking it in that blistering heat of the Permian Basin for weeks on end was what made them mean and rough. And rough wasn't the word for some of those men, and not just around the edges either, I can tell you. Some of their hearts were black as crude.

But they had money, and Mama needed money. She married most of the men that came along, divorced a few, or not, then married a few more. Seemed like to her, marrying was the respectable thing to do. It also seemed like every man that came along left Mama with another mouth to feed, and pretty soon there was a bunch of us–all of us with a different daddy. I was the eldest.

She sometimes talked about her granddaddy and would say, "Eve Marie, that's where you get those strong, high cheek bones from. And when you turn towards the window and the light coming through the shades, I see you are proud like him . . . you carry your pain in silence, baby, too deeply buried to let it knock you down. You're like him. I heard tell he was whupped until he like to bled all his blood out when the rangers finally caught up with him. They said he never dropped his head nor his eyes, not once during that beating. The old folks say his soul shone through those deep amber pools of his eyes. Just like yours, little Eve." She would smile when she said that. "And like you, he could hide his pain, but not the intelligence that maddened the deputies and made them look like a pack of mindless cayotes. Just like you, baby. Strong and smart. You remember that."

Often, maybe too often, those amber pools became a place of refuge not only for me but for other souls in pain,

I thought wryly. But that was okay. I was strong. Apache strong.

~

Being the eldest, I was the one who picked up the pieces of our lives when things went wrong. I remember kneeling beside my mother one night with a wet rag patting the swelling under her eye that some cowboy husband of hers had landed there–right before he cleaned out her purse on his way out the door. We never saw him or the money again.

It seems to me that I must have crawled into her bed that night because I most definitely remember lying there scared, and thinking that somewhere it had to be better than this. And right before daybreak, the dream came again.

The next day, I was the one who went to the church store asking for food for the children because all the money she had was gone. "On its way to New Mexico," Mama said, "with that rough neckin' son of a bitch."

I was just seven years old, and I felt shamed asking for food. But when I thought of Mama's swollen eye, and the other times he'd hurt her, I knew I could be brave enough and old enough for both of us if need be. I was strong. And maybe those sweet smelling' fields would come back into my sleep and I would feel safe again.

Even many years later, I found it hard to talk about. And whenever I did, I could feel myself falling right back into the freezing slush of Brewster County, as it was then. I've heard that since then, some of the oil money trickled in, and more streets were paved, and shacks like ours disappeared. But I haven't gone back to see.

~

That dream stayed with me throughout my childhood and into young adulthood. It kept recurring and even when we left West Texas, it followed me. Wherever we went, didn't matter how hard things got, I knew in my heart, it would never leave me. And I looked forward to that golden refuge full of warm breezes and sweet scents.

And things did get harder. Two more siblings died. One so lost in drugs he didn't know whether he was coming or going in the end. Then, my little sister, on a moving trip through the Rocky Mountains, died of carbon monoxide poisoning when the homemade camper we were in began taking in exhaust from the tail pipe of the truck.

And I dreamed again of the little boy in the grasslands, holding my hand.

Through all of my growing years, I wondered, what was so important that it recurred over and over in that dream across the journey of a lifetime? As I got older I knew it must be some sort of psychological refuge that happened when things got bad. But I was never convinced that it wasn't something more than that. What truth, what warning or premonition was that dream trying to convey as it seeped through the veil between here and what I supposed must be some sort of wonderful place? I would think about it for hours. Never could come up with the answer.

A true field of dreams. It's corny, but that's what it was. And the other thing is, every time I woke up from that dream, I felt so happy. A happiness so deep it would stay with me through the day. It wasn't a sensational sort of dream–just this wonderful feeling of security and peace. And the happiness I felt walking with the boy in the field.

Where are we walking to? I would ask, but no one answered. Towards the place with no edges, I supposed– and then where? Faraway, I hoped, to a place where the pain and the cold and the harshness of my hellish childhood couldn't find me. To somewhere where being happy wasn't just a myth–but something you could see and feel. Not just something people talked about and left you wondering what in the world was 'happiness', anyway. The happy parts of my childhood were few and far between in, I can tell you. But I know what it feels like now and I knew what it felt like back then in that dream.

I still had no idea who the boy was, he didn't look like anyone I knew, or anyone I went to school with, on the days I went to school, or someone I saw at church or anything. He was just a boy. As I got older, I always wondered. I also wondered if the dream was prophetic. I hoped it was. I used to fantasize that it was and that one day it would all come true and I would find myself in that beautiful place and I would know who the boy was. Would I meet him one day in the future?

I had my share of dates as a young woman. Men said I was a 'looker', but that never had the effect it was supposed to. Instead, unlike my mama, I ran the other way, never letting myself get close enough to any man to ever think about marrying him. Mama and my childhood had taken care of that!

But the memory of my dream stayed with me for a long time, and though I kept looking for the boy in every man that came along, he wasn't there. He was nowhere to be found. I began to think nothing like that could ever happen. Not to me.

I finally grew up enough, and got serious enough, about my life to put the dream away–it was happening less and less frequently as the years went by, so it got easier and easier to forget about it. In fact it wasn't long before I stopped thinking about it completely, and the reason for that was that there was something much more important happening in my life, and taking up all my spare thinking time.

I'd met a man. He didn't seem like anything special at the time, and I didn't know what to make of him, but he'd definitely caught my attention.

~

The first time I laid eyes on him, he was sitting on a barstool at the other end of the bar from where I sat on my own barstool, trying to catch the bartenders' eye. Texas men, I was thinking. They have three main interests in life: Pickup trucks, beer and women–in that order. And right now I was sitting on the receiving end of that no account chauvinism. I drummed my fingers on the counter waiting for the conversation between him and a rodeo buck from Abilene to end.

"What do I have to do to get a drink around here? Ride the friggin' bull?" I put my hands on my hips and my eyes wandered down the length of the bar. I'd been here before but had either never noticed the cowboy at the other end or hadn't paid any attention to him if I did.

"Be right with you, darlin'!" Richie Dee drawled as he flipped his grungy bar cloth at a fly on a tall lemonade cooler in the corner.

"Just hope I don't die of thirst before you get here," I retorted.

When I turned my head again, I noticed the man had left his barstool and was walking towards me. He pushed his Stetson back, and scooted the nearest barstool up close to mine.

"I'd like to buy you a drink," he said, holding up a hand to get Richie's attention. As he did so I noticed his watch, which even I recognized as foreign and expensive.

"No need to," I told him, and looked away.

"What're you having?" His manner was sort of cocky as he shifted his weight on the stool and leaned his right elbow on the counter top. In fact his whole self was sort of cocky. Just like a cowboy.

"What are *you* having?" I asked him. I can be cocky too.

He just held my eyes and said, "Jim Beam."

"Me too," I said, and turned away from him to wave to someone I knew back in the shadows of the saloon.

"Jim Beam—twice, please." He told Ricky Dee.

I didn't know whether I liked his cockiness or was turned off by it. So I let it slide. At least we shared a liking for Jim Beam and I remember thinking that was good enough for now.

And then he said. "You married? I'll bet you are. Probably to some perfect man."

The guy was getting a lot too personal and I was mighty uncomfortable with that. So, I took a long swallow of the drink the bar tender put in front of me and said, "I haven't found him yet."

He just put his head back and laughed.

I liked the sound of his laugh. And the funny thing about it was, it broke the edges off the tension between us and we began to talk. Then sometime towards the end of the evening, he asked me to go out with him.

Even after two and a half drinks my defenses went up. I said "No".

And I said "No" the second time he asked me out. I don't think he was used to being turned down, but there was something about this guy I couldn't get too close to. With this one, I knew I'd have to keep my guard up.

His name was Oliver. Classy, I thought. With a name like that he ought to be wearing a silk smoking jacket, holding a cigar in one hand and Jim Beam on the rocks in the other. In actual fact, he was, like me, a product of the oil fields. More likely to smoke a pack of Luckies and carry a six pack of Miller on the front seat of his Ford 150. His face and arms were tanned from the hot Texas sun, he said, and his hair curled around his ears.

The third time he asked me out, I gave in and after we dated for a few months I was seriously beginning to think this relationship might have some potential. It wasn't a crazy-head-over-heels-in-love-at-first-sight sort of thing. Far from it. Oliver wasn't a sweep-me-off-my-feet type of guy–he wasn't DiCaprio, Richard Gere or Tom Selleck sort of guy and nor did he want to be–or so he said. But we laughed a lot. He was funny. Laughter was a big part of us–him and me. We liked the same friends, he was an oil man–which might have been good or bad–and he knew the oil fields, offshore and onshore, so there were no surprises. No explanations necessary. We understood each other and we became friends and lovers in that order.

~

And so it happened one day, without any fanfare, trumpets or drum rolls, Eve and Oliver eloped and, surrounded by a vast expanse of water, were married barefoot in the sand, way down south on Padre Island, hopefully, to live happily ever after.

But nobody was riding off into the sunset just yet.

~

It happened a few years after that lovely wedding on the shores of the Gulf of Mexico that they sat beside another expanse of water, fishing and lazily watching dragon flies swooping and skimming Sabine lake.

The skies were a faded blue color, the way they always are in the summertime in Texas. The water, when Eve dangled her feet over the edge of the creaky wooden dock, was warm and slippery with slimy green weed that grew in trailing swathes around its edges.

There was an old Inn on the knoll above the water, surrounded by trees with limbs as big around as beer barrels. Giant, pre-historic looking limbs that rested on the sandy soil, sheltering the hundred and fifty year old house from the searing afternoon sun and raging spring storms. It was rumored that Sam Houston himself had once slept there.

Oliver sat in a fishing chair with his canvas hat pulled down to shade his eyes, his rod dangling loosely between his knees. "Is that a 'gator in that clump of weed over there?" He asked lazily.

"WHAAA!" Eve pulled her feet out of the water so fast she rolled over onto her back on the warm deck boards. "Where? What 'gator?"

"Never mind. It's gone," he said lazily.

She caught the one-sided grin in the upturn of his mouth. "Oliver, are you kidding me? You're lying, aren't you!" Eve threw her flip flop at him, missing him by a foot as he chuckled and began to reel in his line.

"*Whoa!* Got one!"

"You shouldn't scare me like that, dammit!"

"I just like to see you roll over like you just did—watch out, here he comes! Damn, he's a big 'un!" Oliver gave one last tug, then reached over the dock and with his gloved hand, wrestled a glistening five pounder catfish onto the dock.

Jolie, Eve's childhood friend from Brewster County, lifted herself up on her elbows off the towel she was lying on and pushed her sunglasses up to watch the commotion. "Hmmmph! Not bad." And lay back down.

"Whatd'ya mean 'not bad'?" Oliver feigned hurt.

"Those things are twice that size in Big Lake." She yawned and breathed in the soft, moist air of the East Texas green belt that bordered Louisiana. She was visiting Eve and Oliver and soaking up all the green—trees, grass, and hardwood covered hills—everything they didn't have out west, until it was time to go home tomorrow. "Say, Evie, d'you still have that dream about walkin' through the fields with that little boy–the dream you usta have all the time we were growing up?" She asked, her voice groggy from the sun's heat

"What dream was that?" Oliver, plopped his fish into a nearby bucket and wiped his hands on his shorts.

Eve retrieved her flip flop, slipped it on and sat down beside the fish bucket. "Oh, I had this recurring dream when we were kids. I never knew why. Jolie and I, we used to fantasize about a future happening or maybe even a past life adventure. Anything, so long as it took us out of the oil fields for a while. We all had dreams, didn't we Jolie?" Eve grinned at the thought. "But this one wouldn't go away–not until recently, anyway." She slowly swung around from her perch on the edge of the deck. "Hey! I just realized–that dream hasn't come back for months! That's weird."

She turned to Oliver. "It was a beautiful dream. Soft, light–sort of golden . . . and golden fields that stretched for miles, and me and a little boy walking hand and hand through the long waving grass. Hmmm."

They were all quiet for a moment, each of them lost in the sunshine and tall trees, and the glistening waters of the lake. And then Oliver spoke. "I used to have that dream too, all through my childhood. The exact same dream."

Eve just stared at her husband as he secured his fishing line and propped the rod up against one of the pilings. She couldn't think of anything to say. Her thoughts were freefalling through the years, through all the dreams to this moment.

Finally Jolie spoke.

"I think that you've known each other forever. In spirit, I think." She frowned and swatted a mosquito off the top of her arm. "Darn these things! They're as big as dragonflies around here!"

"What? Spirits?" I teased.

"Now you know that's not what I meant, Eve Marie!" she laughed softly. "Spirits remember. Even though you and Oliver might have forgotten and weren't physically together until a few years ago, I believe your spirits have been together in some way throughout your lives. And maybe even before your lives on earth." She sat up and looked into her childhood friend's eyes. "You've been coming together while you were sleeping for all these years, and helping each other get through the bad times you've gone through. You visited in dreams to remind each other of *what really is*. Spirit visits. I read about that somewhere but I can't recall where."

Eve sat on her beach towel, listening, letting Jolie's words flow through her mind like warm syrup, melting away the years. Oliver was silent.

"I believe that," she finally whispered.

Oliver came and crouched beside her on the deck and looked straight into her eyes. "Me too," he said it so quietly that it made not even a ripple in the warm, moist air. "I haven't had that dream since I met you."

Eve reached up, touched his cheek and said with wonder in her voice, "So it's been you all the time? You're that little boy I've seen all my life . . . and—Oh my God! It's the love we have that brings all those feelings of peace and happiness into the dreams of running through the fields holding hands . . ."

Eve had a funny, faraway look in her eyes. "I had a feeling this could happen, and I know that one day, we'll find ourselves in that dream. We'll be running through those fields for real—where the light is golden and the air shimmers. With you, in a place where we are always young and our hearts are filled with love and peace and beauty."

He smiled at her and said, ". . . or maybe it's happening right now. Just as it is in Heaven."

339

…as it is in Heaven

EPILOGUE

We are the explorers, you and I.

There was a time, back in the '60's and 70's, whenever anyone who wanted to explore their spirituality or find Inner Peace, would set off in the direction of the Far East. Grabbing their saris and sandals, following in the footsteps of The Beatles, they would fly off to Asia for weeks of austerity and discomfort in the Ashrams and sweat boxes of the East.

Others headed out for Spain and the Camino de Santiago, or The Way of St. James, to spend days re-tracing one of the oldest Christian pilgrimages to the shrine of St. James de Compostella. They trekked for 500 miles and more through rugged terrain, in pursuit of enlightenment, sheltering in old inns along the way, and sometimes in a wayside stone shack. Or in a sleeping bag on the stony ground, listening to the sounds of the Spanish night.

It's for sure that some of these experiences achieved their objective and many people came back to the West, calmer, several pounds lighter, and more enlightened than they were when they left. One way or another their eyes would have been opened for better or for worse. I can't help thinking (somewhat blasphemously) that one major benefit might have been the relief they felt when their 'plane landed and they found themselves back in the land of air-conditioning, clean clothes and Micky Dee's. There's nothing like being away for weeks to make one appreciate home like never before. And that's always an enlightening moment.

Many years later, most of us choose to explore the sources and places where inner peace may be found from the comfort of an arm chair in Seattle, Little Rock or Baltimore; or on a swivel chair in front of the computer in the basement of your home.

An interesting follow up might be a trip out west, or to the green strip of eastern Oklahoma, which will lead you into the heart of Native American culture where the folk lore is as rich and deeply colored as the earth. Pathways to inner peace abound. They wind through the wilderness of the Red Rock Canyons of Utah and well-being surrounds you. And it's on our doorstep. More or less

Luckily, there's an even closer place where you can go to find yourself and the spiritual enlightenment you seek. It's found inside each and everyone one of us; and much closer and easier to get to than Tibet, or Kashmir or Bali. Or even the Grand Tetons.

If you're looking for purpose and meaning in your life, try going within, to the deepest part of self. It's the place *you* reside, surrounded by the outer shell that is your human body.

It's that inner voice you sometimes hear and the instincts it generates. It's innate in all of us and you don't have to study transcendentalism or the Sanskrit writings or become a Guru to own it. All you have to do is listen.

Begin by becoming aware of everything around you as if you were seeing or hearing it for the first time. Start with a butterfly circling you, hold out you hand and invite it to alight.

When it does, say "Hi little butterfly, who are you?" The way a child would—even though you might be thinking, It's probably my floral shirt that's attracting it. But then, as you get better at this, the question may become, "Or is it my aura? Did somebody send you as their messenger from the Other Side?"

A child would accept it as just another being in his life. To him it has 'new friend potential'; a beautiful friend, at that. This might be the same child who would turn to the empty space beside him and say, "Did you see that Joey?"

You don't see any "Joey", but he does. And in many cases, it's someone he knows from the place he left to come to earth not so long ago.

The good news is that we, the grown up explorers, can re-start our own curiosity simply by re-aligning our thinking and stepping into that space of saying, "What if?" Then, be still, and allow that acute awareness and acceptance that we had when we were very young, to take root.

Next, you can try to consciously peel away the years. Like peeling an onion, begin by removing the layers that have built up between childhood and today. The first few layers may be hard to pry off. This is because the habits and convictions we've formed over a lifetime have become entrenched. They cling and stick to your fingers, not wanting to move. But recognize them, one by one, and gently move each of them aside to expose the next layer. Before long, you peel back one that reveals a long forgotten open mind. This can be shocking at first but slowly, inch by inch, your exploration of this phenomena begins to make sense as you start to understand its unlimited potential. It's strange, even scary, but, at the very least, it deserves another look. The next layer you peel back may show the way to approaching everything that is 'untypical', 'odd' or seemingly impossible, using that open mind. And as the next few layers drop to the ground, you could find that all the editorializing and judgment you've been hanging onto, goes with it

Allow yourself to float in that space of unblemished wonder. And, just for a moment, remember the way it was all those years ago, when your mind was wide open and pure; and everything around you was waiting to be unwrapped, explored, and gazed at in awe.

Believe that it can be that way again. And if you'd like a travel companion, one who still remembers the way, invite a child to come along.

GB

THE END

Made in the USA
Charleston, SC
02 September 2016